BRUNELLESCHI

in Perspective

THE ARTISTS IN PERSPECTIVE SERIES

H. W. Janson, general editor

The ARTISTS IN PERSPECTIVE *Series presents individual illustrated volumes of interpretive essays on the most significant painters, sculptors, architects, and genres of world art.*

Each volume provides an understanding of art and artists through both esthetic and cultural evaluations.

ISABELLE HYMAN is Associate Professor of Fine Arts at Washington Square College, New York University. Her work has been concentrated on fifteenth-century Florentine architecture. In 1972–73 she was Samuel H. Kress Senior Fellow at Villa I Tatti, The Harvard University Center for Italian Renaissance Studies, in Florence.

BRUNELLESCHI

in Perspective

Edited by

ISABELLE HYMAN

A SPECTRUM BOOK

Prentice-Hall, Inc., Englewood Cliffs, New Jersey

Library of Congress Cataloging in Publication Data

HYMAN, ISABELLE, COMP.
  Brunelleschi in perspective.

  (Artists in perspective series)   (A Spectrum Book)
  Includes bibliographical references.
  1. Brunelleschi, Filippo, 1377–1446.   I. Title.
NA1123.B8H95 1973   720′.92′4   73–12583
ISBN   0–13–084897–2
ISBN   0–13–084889–1 (pbk.)

A SPECTRUM BOOK

1   2   3   4   5   6   7   8   9   10

Printed in the United States of America

PRENTICE-HALL INTERNATIONAL, INC. (LONDON)
PRENTICE-HALL OF AUSTRALIA PTY., LTD. (SYDNEY)
PRENTICE-HALL OF CANADA, LTD. (TORONTO)
PRENTICE-HALL OF INDIA PRIVATE LIMITED (NEW DELHI)
PRENTICE-HALL OF JAPAN, INC. (TOKYO)

ACKNOWLEDGMENTS

I would like to thank the authors and publishers who have given permission to reprint selections from their works, Professor H. W. Janson for his advice and aid, and the other friends and colleagues who have assisted me in assembling this volume. Professor Naomi Miller read the Introduction and made many excellent suggestions for changes and revisions. Help with the Introduction also was given by Professor Marvin Trachtenberg who, in addition, generously contributed some of his previously unpublished photographs. Translations provided by Renate Franciscono, Beverly Levine, and Joan Monahan are individually acknowledged in the text, but I wish to thank the translators here for their help and efficiency. I also received aid with translation from Michele Cone, Gloria Ramakus, and Rhoda Schall. For assistance in the final preparations of the text for publication I am indebted to Lois Granato.

I mention last the person to whom my first and greatest debt of gratitude is due—my husband, Jerome E. Hyman—who gave me the soundest help and advice on every matter, large and small.

CONTENTS

MODERN PERSPECTIVES OF BRUNELLESCHI

BRUNELLESCHI

in Perspective

INTRODUCTION*

Isabelle Hyman

Daedalus was the legendary craftsman, inventor, and artist of the ancient world who constructed the ingenious labyrinth to contain the Cretan minotaur and invented wings of wax so that man could fly. He was renowned for his skills in carpentry, metalwork, architecture, and sculpture, and admiration for his technical ingenuity survived into the Renaissance. The Florentines of the fifteenth century believed that their great and famous architect, Filippo Brunelleschi (1377–1446), was the new Daedalus. When Brunelleschi died they erected in his honor on the wall of Florence Cathedral a monument embellished with his portrait and a Latin epitaph (Fig. 1) which pays tribute to "Filippo the Architect" for his genius in the "Daedalian art." The epitaph was composed by the distinguished state chancellor of Florence, Carlo Marsuppini, who chose to single out from Brunelleschi's many achievements a Daedalus-like ingenuity of such extraordinary inspiration that with it he was able to build the great Cupola (Fig. 6) of the "celebrated temple" in which he was buried. The enormous Dome of Florence Cathedral had grown during the fifteen years (1421–1436) of its construction until it rose "above the skies, ample to cover with its shadow all the Tuscan people," [1] and

---

* In general, footnote references in this Introduction are given only for quotations and works not contained in this volume.

[1] So described by Leon Battista Alberti in his Prologue to *Della Pittura*. See below, p. 27.

1

with it had grown the city's admiration for the architect whose technological wisdom and craftsmanship had made the miracle happen.

Brunelleschi's renown was founded and sustained by this conspicuous and prodigious achievement—the successful construction, without armature,[2] of the illustrious Florentine Dome. Equally extraordinary, however, were his designs for other structures that have become synonymous with the genesis of Renaissance architecture in Italy and his range of accomplishments which, without exaggeration, might be compared to that of Leonardo da Vinci.

Brunelleschi began his career as a goldsmith and sculptor; he went on to invent ingenious machines and mechanical devices and to discover the systematic application of the rules of scientific perspective. He designed and oversaw the construction of ecclesiastical, civic, residential, and military buildings. He was concerned with problems of motion and time (it is reported that he made clocks), statics, hydraulics, mathematics, warfare, naval architecture, and stage production. In the eyes of many contemporaries he was the man who "rediscovered" ancient architecture and thus (as they saw it) restored the lost art of building to its former splendor, binding with pride the Florentines of the fifteenth century to their revered ancestors in the classical world.

During his lifetime Brunelleschi was esteemed not only in Florence but in many other cities of Italy where he was often summoned for consultation and designs. At the time of his death, his supremacy remained unchallenged by any other architect in Italy. The active masters were competent disciples or followers of Filippo's innovative style, and Leon Battista Alberti was just beginning to design the buildings that would make him the only other sovereign figure in the history of Early Renaissance architecture. In fact, the earliest written assessment of Brunelleschi as an artist comes from Alberti, the first writer who, it might be said, put Brunelleschi "in perspective."

In 1435, before Alberti turned to the construction of buildings, he wrote his famous treatise on painting (*De Pictura*) in which he set down the theoretical and practical basis for the art of painting. To the Italian edition of that treatise translated in 1436 from Latin into the vernacular for the benefit of Brunelleschi, he added a pro-

---

[2] Armature: supports for centering traditionally used to hold construction material in place until vault or arch was self-sustaining.

logue dedicated to Brunelleschi that documents their friendship, Alberti's admiration for the Cathedral Dome, and Filippo's fame. It is the earliest contemporary view of Filippo Brunelleschi by a fellow artist who was also a man of acute judgment and intelligence; and in this prologue Alberti named Filippo, along with Donatello, Ghiberti, Luca della Robbia, and Masaccio, as the men in whom "there is a genius for [accomplishing] every praiseworthy thing."

Brunelleschi had enemies as well as admirers. An image of his personality can be pieced together from fragments of documents supplemented by clues from early sources. He was an irascible, argumentative, and secretive man (characteristics that were not inconsistent with the highly competitive atmosphere of early quattrocento Florence). He counseled the Sienese engineer Mariano Taccola to share ideas only with a few people, reportedly saying, "to disclose too much of one's inventions and achievements is one and the same thing as to give up the fruits of one's ingenuity." His biographer, Manetti, reports that Brunelleschi was "fearful of disgrace" and "longed for distinction in whatever he undertook." [3] That he was defiant and independent is attested by records referring to the Stonemasons' and Woodworkers' Guild (*Arte de' Maestri di Pietra e Legnami*), to which he refused to pay an annual fee because of a jurisdictional dispute and, as a result, spent eleven days in jail. That he was vindictive is clear from an incident in which, seeking the aid of no less a personage than the Pope (Eugenius IV), he attempted to force the return of his adopted son, called Buggiano, then a man of twenty-two, from a runaway misadventure in Naples where he had absconded with some of Brunelleschi's money. [4]

Brunelleschi sustained a bitter rivalry with Lorenzo Ghiberti throughout his lifetime, he quarreled with his friend Donatello, and he had acrimonious arguments with Antonio di Manetto Ciaccheri and Giovanni di Gherardo da Prato (among others), men with whom he was associated in architectural projects. But the Florentines were expedient, and Brunelleschi's enmity toward his colleagues and com-

---

[3] Antonio di Tuccio Manetti, *The Life of Brunelleschi,* ed. H. Saalman, trans. C. Enggass (University Park and London, 1970), p. 38.
[4] After this incident Buggiano apparently remained loyal to Brunelleschi until the end of the architect's life. Brunelleschi named him as his heir, and Buggiano carved Brunelleschi's sepulchral effigy at his own expense. See below, pp. 23ff.

petitors did not preclude his collaboration with them on joint projects when it was practical. Those who worked with him found him difficult, perhaps impossible. He could be resentful and rancorous. Sixteenth-century sources report that he smashed to bits his model of a palace for the intimidating Cosimo de' Medici, who dared to criticize it.[5] He had a barbed tongue and was famous for his sarcastic remarks. "What was the best thing Ghiberti ever did," he was asked, according to Vasari. "To sell Lepriano," he supposedly replied, referring to an unproductive piece of real estate.[6]

The antagonism of some of his enemies is recorded in sonnets —a common means for public invective—and surviving too are respondent sonnets by Brunelleschi that sound the notes of righteous self-defense. Giovanni di Gherardo da Prato, critical and scornful of Brunelleschi's projects, particularly his invention of a transport ship (which ultimately did fail), composed a sonnet ridiculing the architect: "O you deep fountain, pit of ignorance, / You miserable beast and imbecile / . . . There is no substance to your alchemy / . . . surely you are mad." These lines elicited from Brunelleschi the oblique but self-confident reply that "For wise men nothing that exists / Remains unseen; . . . / Only the artist, not the fool / Discovers that which nature hides. / Therefore untangle the web of your verses, / Lest they strike sour notes in the dance / When your 'impossible' comes to pass."

Brunelleschi's triumphs vanquished his detractors. Writing his memoirs around 1457, a decade after Brunelleschi's death, Giovanni Rucellai, a wealthy and prominent Florentine citizen, recorded Brunelleschi's place in his chronicle of Florence ("There never was a man more singular in architecture than he"), and set down for the first time one of the most important themes of Brunelleschi literature: that he had rediscovered the building arts of the ancient Romans. A few years later, in 1459, in an anonymous poem eulogizing the Medici family and the greatness of Florence, Brunelleschi's memory

---

[5] *Il Libro di Antonio Billi,* ed. K. Frey (Berlin, 1892), p. 48; repeated by the Anonimo Magliabecchiano, ed. K. Frey (Berlin, 1892), p. 89; and by Giorgio Vasari in *Lives* . . . , Everyman's Library edition (London: J. M. Dent & Sons, Ltd., 1927; New York: E. P. Dutton & Co., Inc., 1927), I, 293.

[6] See below, p. 82.

was honored with three stanzas devoted to his fame; the only other artists mentioned were Cimabue and Giotto. He was granted the rare distinction of burial in the Cathedral of Florence and was publicly lauded by Florentine officials not only for the technical excellence but for the pecuniary economies of his Cupola construction without armature. He was handsomely praised in the architectural treatise written in the early 1460s by the artist Filarete and dedicated to Piero de' Medici: "I bless the soul of Filippo di Ser Brunellesco . . . a famous and most worthy architect, a most subtle follower of Daedalus, who revived in our city of Florence the antique way of building." [7] His name appeared regularly in the lists of preeminent citizens, and he was remembered by later humanist writers like Cristoforo Landino, who praised him for his skill in all the arts, not only in architecture.

Brunelleschi became the first Renaissance artist to be the subject of a full-scale biography, the famous *Vita* written in the 1480s by an anonymous younger admirer now generally identified as Antonio di Tuccio Manetti. Manetti's biography is defensive and prejudiced, but this does not detract from its value as a contemporary account of Brunelleschi's buildings, painted perspective panels, and sculpture, by a man who knew these works and the models, drawings, and documents relating to many of Brunelleschi's projects. Manetti also knew Brunelleschi in his last years. One-sided and often unreliable,[8] the biography established a laudatory approach to Brunelleschi rarely abandoned in subsequent accounts of the artist, which depended heavily on Manetti and on his literary heir, Giorgio Vasari. It is an approach that emphasizes Brunelleschi's fame and versatility, his "renewal" of the lost art of Roman building which made him the initiator of a new epoch in the history of architecture, his besting of all rivals, and the "mistakes" of his followers. Omitted or falsified are the records of inevitable defeats and difficulties borne by every successful person, Brunelleschi not excepted, as we know from more objective and accurate accounts of Florentine history. There is, for

[7] *Filarete's Treatise on Architecture,* Trans., Introd., and Notes by John R. Spencer, New Haven and London, 1965, I, p. 102 (Bk. VIII, fol. 59v).

[8] On the reliability of Manetti as a source, see H. Saalman, ed., Introduction to *The Life of Brunelleschi,* pp. 24ff.

example, Brunelleschi's failure in the planning of marine strategy in the 1430 war between Florence and Lucca, contemptuously described by Giovanni Cavalcanti and later by Machiavelli, the disaster of Brunelleschi's newly invented transport ship recorded in the documents of the Cathedral *Opera*,[9] and of course his defeat in the contest for the Baptistery Door reliefs.

Even with its weaknesses Manetti's *Vita* remains a fundamental source for Brunelleschi studies. It was absorbed thoroughly by Vasari, who augmented it to produce his more elaborate but no less reverential biography of Brunelleschi in the monumental *Vite de' piu eccellenti Architetti, Pittori, et Scultori Italiani . . .* , first published in 1550 and issued in a second and enlarged edition in 1568.

As a source for the history of art probably the most influential book ever written, the *Vite* of Vasari became the foundation of all modern studies of Italian artists. Vasari's biography of Brunelleschi incorporated not only the fifteenth-century Manetti (which remained unpublished until 1812), but earlier sixteenth-century sources such as *Il Libro di Antonio Billi,* which provided information about the architect not found in Manetti. Beyond his accounts of Brunelleschi's works, Vasari's biography is notable for several new features, not all of them commendable. Among the less worthy is Vasari's invention of lengthy and improbable speeches made by Brunelleschi to individuals and assembled citizens about his architectural and sculptural projects. Perhaps because Brunelleschi's peevish and imperious behavior did not conform to Vasari's image of a Florentine hero, the panegyric tone in Vasari's fantasies went beyond that of Manetti and produced a new even-tempered and ingratiating personality for Brunelleschi. Through the ventriloquism of Vasari he became unctuous and priggish and issued sanctimonious and self-complacent statements full of noble but unconvincing sentiments. For example, he conceded the palm of victory to his arch-enemy Lorenzo Ghiberti in the contest for the Baptistery Door because, according to Vasari, he judged Ghiberti's the better work ("This was a true act of friendship, a virtue without envy"). This was instead a most unlikely occurrence, as the astute analysis of Richard Krautheimer in his modern account of the historic competition informs us. And Vasari's statement

---

[9] See F. D. Prager and G. Scaglia, *Brunelleschi, Studies in His Technology and Inventions* (Cambridge, Mass., 1970), pp. 116–19.

about Brunelleschi, that "no one was ever more kind and lovable than he" is controverted by every scrap of contemporary evidence.

Despite its sentimental interpretation of Brunelleschi's character and the invention of implausible orations, Vasari's biography helped perpetuate Brunelleschi's fame and made valuable contributions to the understanding of his work. Vasari discussed the construction of the Barbadori and Ridolfi Chapels as early experiments in the technique of vaulting without armature; he described for the first time, and in elaborate detail, an extraordinary machine invented by Brunelleschi as a stage set for an Annunciation play annually performed in the church of S. Felice in Piazza. He treated the still controversial Palazzo Pitti and the Badia of Fiesole as works by Brunelleschi, and he knew the plan and elevation of S. Maria degli Angeli from a Brunelleschi drawing in his private collection.

Little of significance was added to Brunelleschiana in the seventeenth century, or even in the eighteenth, although the critical attitudes towards the artist started to move in a new direction during those two hundred years. His buildings other than the Cupola began to be ignored in the literature. Only the Cupola continued to be discussed in detail, often as an expression of a chauvinistic rivalry between it and the Dome of St. Peter's in Rome, stimulated by the rise of guidebook literature, or because its size and the mechanical mysteries of its construction continued to elicit reverence and awe. Always in the background, however, loomed the gigantic authority of Vasari's biography, and for that reason the deferential respect (sometimes only lip service) for Brunelleschi's fame and accomplishments was perpetuated.

The seventeenth-century counterpart of Manetti and Vasari was Filippo Baldinucci. His lengthy biography of Brunelleschi made a few new contributions, mostly references to previously unknown events in the artist's life such as his brief term in jail for defying the statutes of the Stonemasons' and Woodworkers' Guild in 1434, but it otherwise relied heavily on Manetti and Vasari. Baldinucci's biography was not published until 1812, when it was brought out by Canon Domenico Moreni in an edition[10] that also included the first publication of the Manetti *Vita* and a long preface in which Moreni elo-

---

[10] D. Moreni, ed., *Vita di Filippo di Ser Brunelleschi architetto fiorentino scritta da Filippo Baldinucci ora per la prima volta pubblicata* . . . (Florence, 1812).

quently attempted to defend Tuscan art and Brunelleschi against the slurs of Francesco Milizia, an important eighteenth-century Italian writer on architecture, which had appeared in the meantime.

Eighteenth-century historians of architecture like Milizia were not interested in the originality of the buildings of fifteenth-century Florence. They demanded a much greater fidelity to the canons of Greco-Roman art than Brunelleschi had demonstrated. They preferred a more rigorous application of the antique orders. The supremacy of the orders and the veneration of Rome dimmed the appreciation of the unorthodox works of Brunelleschi by eighteenth-century classicists, although some gave him credit for being "one of the first architects who gained distinction when the Arts left the shadows where the Barbaric Gothic held them so long enslaved." [11]

Milizia of course included Brunelleschi in *Le Vite de' più celebri architetti* (1768), but he was the first author to strike a significant note of irreverence and criticism toward Brunelleschi as an architect. A Neapolitan who probably had never been to Florence and who certainly did not share Vasari's prejudice in favor of Tuscany, Milizia in his biography of Brunelleschi says of the sacrosanct Cupola that "It is hard to see why the Cupola at Florence should be so much thought of, when those of St. Sophie at Constantinople, St. Mark in Venice, and the Cathedral at Pisa had already been executed." The features of Brunelleschi's career praised by Milizia are his early trips to Rome, reported by Manetti and Vasari, when he (and Donatello) purportedly measured and studied ancient monuments. Brunelleschi also was praised by Milizia for "having first revived the three ancient orders, the Doric, Ionic, and Corinthian." This idea, probably derived by Milizia from the French neoclassical theorist Marc-Antoine Laugier, was based on Vasari's misinterpretation ("[Brunelleschi] reinstated the Tuscan, Corinthian, Doric, and Ionic orders in their original form") of Manetti's statement that Brunelleschi had *studied* all the orders and used "most of them." Anyone, neoclassicist or otherwise, who troubled to look carefully at Brunelleschi's work would discern that he never used the Doric order, that he used the Ionic rarely, and that his "Corinthian" was hardly classical in an archeological sense but was instead his own invention.

[11] J. F. Blondel, *Cours d'architecture* . . . (Paris, 1777), VI, 475.

Milizia was not alone or even original in his appraisal; a few years earlier, in 1765, Laugier in his *Observations Sur l'Architecture* had written about *"Philippe Brunelleschi Florentin, trop peu connu,"* and commended him almost exclusively for restoring *"l'invention des trois ordres grecs."* [12]

When Brunelleschi was admired in the eighteenth century, then, it was not for the unique quality of his architectural style, which was not understood and appreciated, or for his accomplishments in sculpture and scientific perspective, which apparently were forgotten. Brunelleschi literature in that century and the one that followed consisted often of little more than a partial chronicle of his activities or superficial references to some of his buildings. The former became a series of fables, and the latter a repetitive litany of routine praise without analysis or interpretation. Brunelleschi's fame depended almost exclusively on the idea, originating in literature with Rucellai and Manetti, of his having released architecture from a dark imprisonment in the Middle Ages, from *"les ténèbres de la Barbarie."* [13]

Any image of Brunelleschi as the artist who restored at least some features of the classical style of architecture had to be incomplete and deceptive. It ignored the much more perceptive view expressed well before Manetti in the few paragraphs of Alberti's Prologue to *Della Pittura.* For all of Alberti's veneration of antique culture and Roman architecture, he appreciated and praised Brunelleschi for his *modern* achievements, for the *new* things he was doing ("we [of this era] discover unheard-of and never-before-seen arts and sciences without teachers or without any model whatsoever"). Alberti pointed out that what Brunelleschi had achieved with the Cupola was all the more wonderful because he had *not* had a precedent in antiquity ("unknown and unthought of among the ancients"). Alberti had recognized and expressed what Brunelleschi was most celebrated for in his own lifetime—his ingenuity, his originality, and his technological innovations: "You [Brunelleschi] persevere in discovering things through which your extraordinary genius acquires perpetual fame." It was Manetti who, some fifty years after Alberti, strove to cement the connections between Brunelleschi and antiquity with accounts of the

[12] M.-A. Laugier, *Observations Sur l'Architecture,* facsimile reprint of first edition of 1765 (Farnborough, Hants.: Gregg International Press, Ltd., 1966), pp. 77f.
[13] *Ibid.,* p. 78.

archeological expeditions to Rome, and his revival of the orders and of Roman masonry work. Not that Manetti had neglected Brunelleschi's ingenuity, but he was more enthusiastic about his "classicism."

Manetti's account of Brunelleschi as the initiator of a new epoch in the history of architecture had been reasserted by Vasari in his Introduction to Part II of the *Vite*: ". . . by means of the study and diligence of the great Filippo Brunelleschi, architecture once again discovered the measurements and proportions of the ancients." [14] Yet from Vasari's point of view the art of the fifteenth century represented only the second stage of an art that did not come to full development until the High Renaissance. He saw the Renaissance as ripening from humble beginnings around 1250 ("the age of childhood") to "the perfection of the third age," the sixteenth century. [15] To Vasari, the artists of the fifteenth century, admire them as he did, still belonged to the tentative stage that preceded the consummate achievement of the cinquecento.

It was this approach that was adopted and embellished in the nineteenth century by Heinrich Wölfflin and his disciples. Wölfflin, the Swiss art historian who succeeded Jacob Burckhardt in the Chair of Art History at Basel in 1893, saw the fifteenth century as an "early" Renaissance with Florence as its birthplace and Brunelleschi its father. He wrote of a development from the "immature and playful flexibility" of fifteenth-century architecture to the "mature, measured, and severe" style of the sixteenth. [16] An eloquent attempt to assail this evolutionary history of Renaissance architecture, most cogently espoused by Wölfflin, was made in 1914 by Geoffrey Scott in *The Architecture of Humanism*. Attacking what he called the "biological fallacy," Scott sought to release Renaissance architecture from the "values of biology" and Brunelleschi from the consequent image of him as "struggling . . . after an ideal which later was fulfilled." Scott claimed that "[Brunelleschi's] architecture was not Bramante's unachieved, but his own fulfilled."

The "evolutionists" like Wölfflin represented one path through the tangled thicket of late nineteenth-century critical thought, and

[14] G. Vasari, *Lives*, ed. cit., I, 207.
[15] *Ibid.*
[16] H. Wölfflin, *Classic Art, an Introduction to the Italian Renaissance,* trans. Peter and Linda Murray from the 8th German edition (London, 1961), p. 286.

the Victorians of sentimental persuasion another. Devoted to what Mary McCarthy calls "a tooled-leather idea of Florence as a dear bit of the old world," [17] they complacently accepted as gospel Vasari's fictionalization of Brunelleschi's character and his anecdotal account of the architect's life. Translated into German, French, and English for the first time in the nineteenth century, Vasari's *Vite* were adapted in England and America into numerous quaint biographies, [18] and later even into dramatic monologues in verse, [19] which depended entirely on Vasari and further misinterpreted his already sentimental profile of Brunelleschi. Even the serious historians of architecture who wrote earlier in the nineteenth century, such as Quatremère di Quincy, had slavishly repeated Vasari and skillfully embroidered his anecdotes with the lingering threads of neoclassicism. They emphasized above all the accounts of Brunelleschi's role as the initiator of the new epoch, and the importance of his early Roman experiences, the length, impact, and veracity of which they did not doubt.

Also during this century of complex critical thought there developed another vein of criticism, heavily infused with the spirit of John Ruskin and his American followers such as Charles Eliot Norton and Charles Herbert Moore. It concentrated on extolling and idealizing the character of medieval art, and especially architecture. Believing in a correspondence between Christian morality and art, Ruskin and his disciples understood medieval art to be Christian and therefore moral, whereas in their view Renaissance art, because it

[17] M. McCarthy, *The Stones of Florence* (New York, n.d.), p. 10.
[18] For example, *The Makers of Florence* by Mrs. [Margaret] Oliphant (London, 1876): "Filippo of Ser Brunellescho of the Lapi, which is, according to Florentine use, his somewhat cumbrous name, or Brunelleschi *tout court*, as custom permitted him to be called, was the son of a notary who, as notaries use, hoped and expected his boy to follow in his steps and succeed to his practice. But like other sons doomed their fathers' soul to cross, Filippo took to those *figuretti* in bronze which were so captivating to the taste of the time, and preferred rather to be a goldsmith, to hang upon the skirts of art, than to work in the paternal *bottega*." From pp. 136f. of the 1908 edition.
[19] For example, *Brunelleschi, a Poem*, by John Galen Howard (San Francisco, 1913): [Brunelleschi is speaking] "Ha! Arnolfo, how would you / Lift eyes in prayer could you but see this heaven / I've crowned your space withal! Could you forgive / In jealousy for thine own striving hand, / My bettering your best? / . . . Naught greater God hath created than my blushing Dome / The virgin breast of Florence! . . . / Most of all from him (high heart) my fountains take their rise / Who first laid down the pregnant octagon / . . ."

was "pagan," was amoral. In opposition to the neoclassicists those evangelical critics who did admire Brunelleschi saw him not in his time-honored role as the reviver of antiquity—since the revival of antiquity was deplored—but as the last breath of the venerated but expiring medieval traditions of architecture. They praised the Cupola for its pointed profile and its integral relationship to the Gothic basilica it crowned, and for the fourteenth-century origins of its design; but they had little or nothing to say about Brunelleschi's other structures with their more obvious Renaissance characteristics. Charles Herbert Moore, colleague of Charles Eliot Norton at Harvard and first director of the Fogg Art Museum, published *Character of Renaissance Architecture* in 1905, after writing many studies of medieval architecture. The book embodies the Ruskinian attitude towards the Renaissance as amoral, pagan, and dishonest. Moore praised Brunelleschi's Cupola for its "beauty of outline," but criticized it vehemently for "its departure from sound methods of dome construction." He displaced the traditional awe and admiration for Brunelleschi's technical virtuosity with disdain for his engineering methods and workmanship, a reversal of the fifteenth- and sixteenth-century perspective of Brunelleschi as *"architetto della stupenda macchina della cupola,"* as Francesco Bocchi described him in 1591. As for other buildings by Brunelleschi, Moore dismissed them with a few lines: "None of his other opportunities were such as to call forth his best powers. . . . In these other works he revives the use of the orders and employs them in modes which for incongruity surpass anything that imperial Roman taste had devised."

Ruskin wrote mainly about Venetian Gothic architecture in order to demonstrate what he believed to be "the most interesting facts of architectural history," [20] and because "it is in Venice, therefore, and in Venice only, that effectual blows can be struck at this pestilent art of the Renaissance." [21] He had little to say about Brunelleschi, not only because of his concentration on architecture outside of Florence and before the Renaissance but, one suspects, because he had trouble fitting Brunelleschi into moral categories of art. However, in *The Seven Lamps of Architecture* (1849), although inveighing against the use of metal in architecture, Ruskin grudgingly deferred to

[20] J. Ruskin, *The Seven Lamps of Architecture*, 4th ed. (Kent, 1883), p. xviii.
[21] *Idem., The Stones of Venice*, 4th ed. (Kent, 1886), Ch. I, Sec. xxxix.

Brunelleschi: ". . . neither can we well deny to the Gothic architect the power of supporting statues, pinnacles, or traceries by iron bars; and if we grant this I do not see how we can help allowing Brunelleschi his iron chain around the dome of Florence." The statement suggests, among other things, that Ruskin did not understand Brunelleschi's method of chain construction, that he envisioned a series of metal links girdling the double shell of the Cupola instead of the complex system (still the subject of debate) contrived of wood and stone as well as iron.[22]

Around the same mid-century years in England, James Fergusson, Scottish archeologist and writer on architecture, published his popular and influential *The Illustrated Handbook of Architecture* (1855), and in the Preface he wrote: "One great division of art still remains to be described. . . . It is that style which arose in the middle of the fifteenth century, culminated with the rebuilding of St. Peter's at Rome, and has prevailed all over Europe during the last three centuries and a half. It is infinitely inferior to the Gothic, which preceded it, as an artistic form of art, but nearly as important from the size and splendour of the buildings in which it is employed. . . ." [23] His discussion of that style appeared in his *History of the Modern Styles of Architecture* (1862) in a brief section entitled "Churches Anterior to St. Peter's," which devotes its few pages to Brunelleschi and Alberti.[24]

The attitude towards Brunelleschi in Italy and Germany during the nineteenth century was altogether different from that of the English and American critics. On the Continent the Italian Renaissance was approached with deference and respect. There critics employed scientific historicism instead of basing judgments solely on moral or aesthetic standards. Using the apparatus of historical and scientific methodology, art historians and archivists began to look at the art of the Renaissance in Italy from the perspective of historical analysis. It was from this direction that serious modern understanding of the Italian Renaissance in general and Brunelleschi in particular emerged.

[22] Compare Prager and Scaglia, *op. cit.*, pp. 34–37 and the review by H. Saalman, *Journal of the Society of Architectural Historians*, XXXI, 1972, pp. 241f.

[23] J. Fergusson, *The Illustrated Handbook of Architecture* (London, 1855), pp. viii–ix.

[24] *Idem.*, *History of the Modern Styles of Architecture,* 2nd. ed. (London, 1873), pp. 43ff.

If we look for a convenient starting point, we might find it in 1839–40 with the publication of the Danish archivist Giovanni Gaye's *Carteggio inedito* . . . ,[25] a collection containing new and useful documents relating to the lives and careers of Italian Renaissance artists, including Brunelleschi. In 1857 and 1887, Cesare Guasti, Superintendent of the Archives of Tuscany, published two invaluable volumes of documents extracted from the archives of the *Opera* of the Cathedral of Florence recording details of the construction of the church and its Cupola.[26] This information about the course of that monumental work greatly enlarged the knowledge of Brunelleschi's technology and of his role at the Cathedral. From 1878 to 1885 the erudite archivist Gaetano Milanesi published his annotated edition of the Vasari *Vite*[27] containing extensive new sources and documents, and in 1887 he published a new edition of Manetti's *Vita*.[28] Beginning in 1885, Carl von Stegmann and Heinrich von Geymüller published measured drawings of Brunelleschi's buildings[29] that were so meticulously made that architectural historians had the chance to see things that hardly had been visible to the naked eye; they could analyze Brunelleschi's use of proportions, and relate individual parts of plan and elevation to the total complex of the building.

Drawing on all available sources and documents plus his own far-reaching and imaginative archival researches, Cornel von Fabriczy in 1892 published his unsurpassed monograph, *Filippo Brunelleschi, Sein Leben und Seine Werke*, and supplemented this work with additional material published in an article in 1907.[30] Fabriczy's exhaustive studies of Brunelleschi contained the most punctiliously compiled information about Brunelleschi's personal life and professional career

[25] G. Gaye, *Carteggio inedito d'artisti*. . . . *Documenti di Storia Italiana* (Florence, 1839).
[26] C. Guasti, *La Cupola di Santa Maria del Fiore* (Florence, 1857); and *Santa Maria del Fiore. La Costruzione della Chiesa e del Campanile* (Florence, 1887).
[27] G. Vasari, *Le Vite de' piu eccellenti architetti, pittori, scultori italiani* (Florence, 1568), ed. G. Milanesi (Florence, 1878–1885).
[28] G. Milanesi, ed., *Operette istoriche edite ed inedite di Antonio Manetti* . . . (Florence, 1887).
[29] C. v. Stegmann and H. v. Geymüller, *Die Architektur der Renaissance in Toskana*, Vol. I (Munich, 1885–1893).
[30] C. v. Fabriczy, "Brunelleschiana," *Jahrbuch der Preuszischen Kunstsammlungen*, 28 (1907), Beiheft, 1ff.

that had ever been assembled. With Fabriczy's studies the machinery of modern art historical investigation was put into full gear.

A torrent of literature, which even at present shows no sign of ebbing, devoted mostly or exclusively to Brunelleschi studies followed Fabriczy. Scholars have explored through archeology, archival research, and intensive stylistic analysis the history of individual buildings. Studies have been devoted exclusively to Brunelleschi's use of proportion, to his discovery of scientific perspective, to the extent of his technological and scientific knowledge, to the structural scheme of all of his buildings, not only the Cupola, and to the reconstruction of aborted projects. Many new facts have been revealed to challenge rooted ideas about structures like the portico of the Pazzi Chapel, the vaulting of the nave of S. Spirito, and the original shape of the exterior walls and the facade of that church. Attributions to Brunelleschi of the Palazzo Pitti, the Badia in Fiesole, and the Barbadori Chapel of S. Felìcita, have been convincingly proposed by some scholars and equally convincingly denied by others, in the absence of definitive documents. Brunelleschi's stage machinery, his inventions of machines for architectural construction, his writings, and his sculpture—all have been the subject of serious scholarly attention.[31]

Attitudes towards the relationship between Brunelleschi and the antique have constituted a pervasive and persistent theme in critical literature from the time of Alberti. Perspectives have shifted continually. As we have already noted, to Alberti, Brunelleschi's achievement was in his originality, his lack of dependence on antiquity; but to Manetti and Vasari, Brunelleschi's comprehension and assimilation of the lost greatness of Roman architecture resulted in the epoch of the Renaissance.

Later critics, writing from the mid-eighteenth century on, who admired the work of neoclassic architects, were bewildered by these previous commendations of Brunelleschi's classicism, for in their eyes his architecture had none of the grandeur and canonical perfection that they associated with the respected Greco-Roman style. Yet others,

---

[31] Although of value and interest, most of these studies are too technical in treatment or too restricted in scope to be reprinted in this collection of more general "perspectives." For a full bibliography through 1971 see my biography of Brunelleschi in *Dizionario Biografico degli Italiani*, 14, Rome, 1972, pp. 542–544.

like Ruskin, who were inspired and moved not by antiquity but by the "magnificently human" Gothic architecture of the twelfth and thirteenth centuries found Brunelleschi too classical for their taste and censured him for betraying the traditions of medieval art. Further contradictory currents emerged during the nineteenth century: one, emanating from the ideas of Wölfflin, saw Brunelleschi as a "father of the Renaissance" [32] because of his *all'antica* manner which, even though regarded as immature, was considered to be the ancestor of the High Renaissance, or classic Renaissance, style. Another, first proposed by G. Dehio in 1886 [33] and which quickly gathered many supporters, claimed that Brunelleschi's artistic roots were not to be found in the architecture of Rome after all, but rather in the Romanesque structures abounding in Tuscany—buildings like the Baptistery and S. Miniato in Florence, the facade of the Badia in Fiesole, the Collegiata in Empoli.

In 1893, Paola Fontana, following Dehio, contested vigorously the idea of the antique as the main source of Brunelleschi's style (although he felt he had to apologize for doing so). He was deeply sceptical of Manetti's and Vasari's accounts of the importance and length of Brunelleschi's early Roman sojourn, and he seriously challenged the hitherto inviolable and unquestioned authority of the early biographers. He set out to prove through an analysis and comparison of architectural details that Brunelleschi's genius had developed from his careful observation of Romanesque buildings in Florence and its environs, even though Fontana judged the style of those buildings to be "imperfect" when compared to those of antiquity.

Other writers, like Fabriczy in 1892 and Folnesics in 1915, in their monographic studies of Brunelleschi sought to subordinate the question of Brunelleschi's architectural antecedents and instead to draw out from their analyses of his buildings the originality of his inventions and his freedom from architectural formulae. "[Brunel-

---

[32] For a later expression of this theme see M. Dvořák, *Geschichte der Italienischen Kunst im Zeitalter der Renaissance*, I, Munich, 1927, Ch. II, "Die Patres der Renaissance," pp. 15ff.

[33] G. Dehio, "Romanische Renaissance," *Jahrbuch der Preuszischen Kunstsammlungen*, VII (1886), pp. 129ff.

leschi's] genius sprang fully developed from the master's own mind," claimed Fabriczy. Although Folnesics recognized that the Cupola represented Brunelleschi's "greatest engineering feat," he did not include a discussion of it in his study, because its shape, having been determined in the fourteenth century, "had nothing to do with [Brunelleschi's] work as an artist." According to Folnesics, "Only by looking at the buildings he created without influence, with free hands, can we get to know the artist." Despite these points of view there were still in the first two decades of the twentieth century many attempts by historians of art like Bode, Willich, and Schmarsow to assess the relationship of Brunelleschi's architecture to the Middle Ages or to antiquity.[34] Since that time the pendulum between the classical Brunelleschi and the medieval Brunelleschi has been swinging vigorously back and forth, its momentum derived from differing opinions about the dependence of Brunelleschi on models from ancient and medieval architecture, and from the desire to establish a clear definition of Brunelleschi's architectural style.

The first significant analysis of the style of Brunelleschi's late works was made in 1931 by Ludwig H. Heydenreich. Describing the architectural forms in terms of an increasing density and mass, Heydenreich traced this development from a planar wall architecture in a group of Brunelleschi's early structures including the Old Sacristy and S. Lorenzo, to a plastic mode of expression in the late buildings of S. Maria degli Angeli, S. Spirito, and the Exedrae of the Cathedral. In the heavy forms and powerful profiles of the late structures Heydenreich perceived an indirect relationship to precedents in Roman architecture which Brunelleschi assimilated rather than copied to form his new, and original, style.

A recent study by Heinrich Klotz analyzes the early work of Brunelleschi.[35] While earlier writers like Dehio and Fontana had discovered connections between Brunelleschi and Romanesque buildings of the eleventh and twelfth centuries, Klotz explores the relation of Brunelleschi's early works to the architecture of the Late Gothic period,

[34] Summarized by Emil Kaufmann, *Architecture in the Age of Reason*, Cambridge (Mass.), 1955, pp. 79f.
[35] H. Klotz, *Die Frühwerke Brunelleschis und der Mittelalterliche Tradition*, Berlin, 1970.

the fourteenth century in Italy. Another recent contribution to the question of antique and post-antique works as sources for Brunelleschi's architecture can be found in an interesting essay by Howard Burns.[36] While acknowledging the "generic antique inspiration" [37] of Brunelleschi's new style, Burns claims that "there is not a single major work of Brunelleschi for which a plausible and specific post-antique source (or sources) cannot be suggested." [38] The work of Klotz and Burns demonstrates the continued honing and refining of the complex subject of influences on the development of Brunelleschi's style. Other contemporary historians of architecture have chosen to attack this problem by focusing attention on the details of Brunelleschi's architecture rather than on the large fabrics. A prime example of this approach is Howard Saalman's intensive and systematic study of the forms of Brunelleschi's capitals. Saalman's analysis reveals that for the most part Brunelleschi's capitals are not dependent on genuine antique prototypes or on the classicizing capitals found in Tuscan Protorenaissance architecture. They are based instead on Brunelleschi's original reworking of elements in Tuscan Romanesque and Gothic capitals that were not imitations of those of antiquity. Some influence from antique prototypes can be found, according to Saalman, "only in Brunelleschi's latest period."

The notion of a "late period" for Brunelleschi, and the interpretation by Heydenreich of a correspondence between indirect classical prototypes and the development of plastic form in Brunelleschi's late works, were challenged in 1964 by Eugenio Luporini in his *Brunelleschi: Forma e Ragione*.[39] Studying the works of Brunelleschi in a new light, Luporini has denied any "isolation of Brunelleschi's late activity." [40] By analyzing all the buildings as one unit, not serially or chronologically since many of them were simultaneously in one phase of construction or another during Brunelleschi's lifetime, Luporini perceives a development towards maturity within *each* work rather

---

[36] H. Burns, "Quattrocento Architecture and the Antique: Some Problems," *Classical Influences on European Culture A.D. 500–1500*, ed. R. R. Bolgar, Cambridge, 1971, pp. 269–287, esp. pp. 279ff.

[37] *Ibid.*, p. 283.

[38] *Ibid.*, p. 277.

[39] E. Luporini, *Brunelleschi: Forma e Ragione*, Milan, 1964.

[40] *Ibid.*, p. 24.

than in what is to him a falsely separated early and late style. The architectural plasticity of antiquity is found, according to Luporini, not in Brunelleschi's work, but rather in the buildings of the architects who followed him in the next generation.[41]

In fact, the whole question of the relationship of Brunelleschi's architecture, and its innovations, to architecture in Italy (and not only in Florence) in the decades after his death has been probed very little. Sorting out Brunelleschi's artistic predecessors instead of his successors has been a major concern for most critics. In 1962, Piero Sanpaolesi, however, opened a new door with his refreshing and sensitive literary portrait of Brunelleschi, in which he traced the migration of Brunelleschi's architectural forms to Lombardy and Emilia, where they are found in works by Alessio Tramello and others. And while the importance for art history of establishing Brunelleschi's ties to the past and to the future cannot be disputed, Sanpaolesi has also reminded us of Brunelleschi's artistic freedom and of the uniqueness of his creative gift. His individuality defies categorization and eludes definitive analysis; at the same time it remains continually stimulating. Although many recent studies of Brunelleschi have not abandoned the historic search for a definition of his style, they have tended to concentrate less on this problem and more on the exploration of his "Daedalian" genius and on his scientific and technological skills. Brunelleschi as a craftsman and engineer, his technological inventions, the structure of the Cupola, are the subjects of the investigations of Frank D. Prager and Gustina Scaglia, many now compiled into one volume, *Brunelleschi, Studies of his Technology and Inventions.* The authors analyze technical documents and drawings of machinery, and discuss the influence of Brunelleschi's technology as well as defining, within the context of this technology, the persistent problem of his relation to the classic and Gothic worlds.

Brunelleschi's development of perspective theory has been explained by Richard Krautheimer as a pragmatic architectural tool for drawing buildings to scale. It was Krautheimer's insight to realize that although Brunelleschi's linear perspective method was eventually adopted by painters and sculptors, it was "devoted to the representa-

[41] *Ibid.*, p. 25.

tion of architecture" when it was first invented and that Brunelleschi had "proceeded along lines strictly architectural in thought."

The collection of documents, sources, and essays on Brunelleschi that follows this Introduction was selected to offer the reader a variety of viewpoints within a wide historical range. From this "critical panorama" it is possible to see how Brunelleschi's achievements have stimulated critical minds for over five hundred years, and how each age has attempted to challenge his elusiveness with its own intellectual weapons. Thus one of the latest studies of Brunelleschi's work (which because of its mathematical nature is not reprinted here) seems oddly appropriate to our own time. It is a new attempt to penetrate the mysteries of the construction of the Cupola of Florence Cathedral through a photogrammetric survey in which the calculation of the curvature of the inner and outer shells of the Cupola was made with the ultimate of modern research—the electronic computer.[42] Yet no sooner were the conclusions published than they were challenged.[43] Apparently not even the ingenuity of the computer is a match for the invincible "gifts and virtues" [44] of Brunelleschi's mind.

[42] W. Ferri, M. Fondelli, P. Franchi, F. Greco, "Il Rilevamento Fotogrammetrico della Cupola di S. Maria del Fiore in Firenze," *Bollettino di Geodesia e Scienze affini*, Fasc. N. 3, 1971.

[43] P. Sanpaolesi and G. Birardi, "Vecchie e Recenti Ricerche Sulla Cupola di Santa Maria del Fiore e la Interpretazione di un Nuovo Rilievo Fotogrammetrico," *Antichità Viva*, XI, no. 2, 1972, pp. 39f. Called to my attention by Dr. Howard Saalman. Now see M. Fondelli, "Lettera al Direttore," *Antichità Viva*, XI, n. 5, 1973, pp. 85f.

[44] From Brunelleschi's epitaph, see below, p. 24.

FUNERAL HONORS FOR BRUNELLESCHI

Consuls of the *Wool Guild*
(Arte Della Lana) *of Florence*
Provision of December 30, 1446 *

The abovementioned noble consuls in turn assembled in the audience hall of the guild palace as is their usual custom. Reports made by numerous merchants and artisans of the guild and by other knowledgeable citizens were heard, maintaining that Filippo Brunelleschi, an honorable Florentine citizen, expended his efforts with the greatest diligence and ingenuity in the building and construction of the Cupola of the Cathedral of Santa Maria del Fiore in Florence, and in the final planning for the construction of the Lantern of the Cupola, and in the Tribunes, and in many other works at this church for so many years; and that by his careful economy the greatest expenses that it would have been fitting for his genius and intelligence to make were removed; and that those things mentioned above have

---

* The Wool Guild was responsible for the construction and decoration of the Cathedral of Florence, Santa Maria del Fiore, and for other Cathedral matters as, for example, its use as a burial place for special and distinguished citizens such as Brunelleschi. The Latin text of this provision and of the one following are found in C. Guasti, *La Cupola di Santa Maria del Fiore* (Florence, 1857), p. 55, doc. 119; p. 56, doc. 120. Translations by Joan Monahan.

been demonstrated by experience, and that it would be as fitting for the honor and fame of Filippo as for the honor of all Florence that gratitude be shown, most especially by the guild on whose behalf he expended himself in these works with all care, diligence, and skill. And this seemed fitting and pleased the consuls. Wishing to make arrangements for this because of the reasons mentioned above, after the customary deliberation in turn on each and every point mentioned above and below the usual secret vote was taken with white and black beans, and the result obtained according to the regulations of the guild, it was provided, advised, and ordained: that the consuls of the guild together with the administrators or overseers of the Cathedral Works, a two-thirds majority even with some absent or unpolled or present and dissenting, from this time through the entire coming month of February, and within that time and deadline, must do whatever they can by themselves or through those to whom they entrust this matter, to take care of, arrange, and order in what place in the church and under what circumstances the body of Filippo Brunelleschi shall be buried and put to rest, and on that account to allot as much marble from the Cathedral Works as is necessary for the construction and sculpture [of his tomb] at the expense of Filippo's heir [Andrea di Lazzaro Cavalcanti] or his successors, and not in any way at the expense of the Cathedral Works. And also for [Brunelleschi's] honor they are to designate a place in the church and to see that inscribed there are fitting verses and lines as seem best and pleasing to them in a way respecting the honor of all Florence, the guild, and the man himself. With no one objecting etc.

Overseers of the Works
of Florence Cathedral
Provision of February 18, 1447 *

The noble and wise men, overseers of the Works of Florence Cathedral, together with Battista Arnolfi and Piero di Cardinale Rucellai, to whom through the resolutions of the Wool Guild was entrusted the responsibility for the honors to be given the body of a most eloquent and ingenious man, Filippo Brunelleschi, Florentine citizen, for many years *capomaestro* of the Cupola and Lantern of the Cathedral, through whose work, industry, and skill with the help of God and the Virgin Mary the great dome was completed without armature as the overseers clearly testify and as is seen and noted in the city, wishing to provide for the honors to be given to his body and for his perpetual fame with due measures being taken unanimously and with one voice have advised and ordained: that the body of Filippo, up to this time buried and laid to rest in the Campanile, be taken from that location and placed in the church, specifically in the floor at that place where the oath is given to the principal magistrates, about in the center and deeply [buried]; and below this brick floor, once it has been repaved, let nothing appear except a slab of marble on which should be inscribed FILIPPUS ARCHITECTOR,[1] and a cover built over it, namely in the shape of an arch. And on the wall near the place where his body will be buried, namely in the first wall

---

* [1446 Florentine Style—Ed.]

[1] [Brunelleschi's tomb was uncovered for the first time in July, 1972, during the excavation of the foundations of Santa Reparata, the old church above which the present Cathedral of Florence was built. The inscription on the marble slab (Fig. 2) departs from the simple designation in the document and reads: CORPUS MAGNI INGENII VIRI PHILIPPI SER BRUNELLESCHI FLORENTINI (The Body of a Man of Great Genius Filippo di Ser Brunelleschi Florentine). —Ed.]

lunette, will be placed a stone or some marble (Fig. 1) on which there should be his image *al naturale* with some of the designs that he invented or used in the completion of the Cupola. And in addition to this, let some verses be inscribed for his perpetual fame and honor depicting his diligence and skill in architecture, and they will be composed and set down by the famous lord Carlo Marsuppini chancellor of Florence; they are to be constructed and placed on the face of the wall. It was declared that the Cathedral Works will provide as much marble as necessary and workmen for accomplishing these things; and [Brunelleschi's] heirs are to see to all else for the burial of his body.

Carlo Marsuppini (1398–1453)

Epitaph Commemorating
Brunelleschi

How Filippo the Architect excelled in the Daedalian art not only this celebrated temple with its marvelous shell but also the many machines his divine genius invented can document. Wherefore because of the distinguished singular gifts and virtues of his mind on the XV of April in the year MCCCCXLVI[1] a grateful country decreed that his deserving body be buried in this grave.

The epitaph is a part of the wall monument in Florence Cathedral (Fig. 1) honoring Brunelleschi. Translated from the Latin text published in Guasti, *Cupola,* 1857, p. 57, doc. 121.

---

[1] [The date of Brunelleschi's death. Until the deliberations and preparations for his burial site and sepulchre resulted in his interment beneath the Cathedral at the end of May, 1447, his body was kept temporarily in the Campanile. See p. 23. —Ed.]

Francesco Bocchi (*1548–1618*)
Comment on Brunelleschi's
Monument in Florence Cathedral
(1591)

... on the right side near the door one sees the statue of Filippo Brunelleschi who was the architect of the stupendous construction that is the Cupola, and in memory of such sovereign industry [his statue] was gladly put up by the people in this notable place.

Translated from F. Bocchi, *Le bellezze della citta di Fiorenza* (Florence, 1591); republished in facsimile by Gregg International Publishers (Farnborough, Hants., England, 1971), p. 22.

OTHER EARLY SOURCES
AND DOCUMENTS

Leon Battista Alberti (1404–1472)
Prologue to *On Painting* (1436)

I used to marvel and at the same time to grieve that so many excellent and superior arts and sciences from our most vigorous antique
past could now seem lacking and almost wholly lost. We know from
[remaining] works and through references to them that they were
once widespread. Painters, sculptors, architects, musicians, geometri-
cians, rhetoricians, seers and similar noble and amazing intellects are
very rarely found today and there are few to praise them. Thus I
believed, as many said, that Nature, the mistress of things, had grown
old and tired. She no longer produced either geniuses or giants which
in her more youthful and more glorious days she had produced so
marvellously and abundantly.

Since then, I have been brought back here [to Florence]—from
the long exile in which we Alberti have grown old—into this our city,

From Leon Battista Alberti, *On Painting*, rev. ed., translated with Introduction
and Notes by John R. Spencer (New Haven: Yale University Press, and London:
Routledge & Kegan Paul, Ltd., 1970), pp. 39–40. Reprinted without the footnotes
by permission of the publishers. This Prologue did not appear in the Latin original
of the treatise (1435) but in Alberti's own Italian translation of 1436. See above,
pp. 2ff.

adorned above all others. I have come to understand that in many men, but especially in you, Filippo, and in our close friend Donato the sculptor and in others like Nencio, Luca and Masaccio,[1] there is a genius for [accomplishing] every praiseworthy thing. For this they should not be slighted in favour of anyone famous in antiquity in these arts. Therefore, I believe the power of acquiring wide fame in any art or science lies in our industry and diligence more than in the times or in the gifts of nature. It must be admitted that it was less difficult for the Ancients—because they had models to imitate and from which they could learn—to come to a knowledge of those supreme arts which today are most difficult for us. Our fame ought to be much greater, then, if we discover unheard-of and never-before-seen arts and sciences without teachers or without any model whatsoever. Who could ever be hard or envious enough to fail to praise Pippo the architect on seeing here such a large structure, rising above the skies, ample to cover with its shadow all the Tuscan people, and constructed without the aid of centering or great quantity of wood? Since this work seems impossible of execution in our time, if I judge rightly, it was probably unknown and unthought of among the Ancients. But there will be other places, Filippo, to tell of your fame, of the virtues of our Donato, and of the others who are most pleasing to me by their deeds.

As you work from day to day, you persevere in discovering things through which your extraordinary genius acquires perpetual fame. If you find the leisure, it would please me if you should look again at this my little work On Painting which I set into Tuscan for your renown. You will see three books; the first, all mathematics, concerning the roots in nature which are the source of this delightful and most noble art. The second book puts the art in the hand of the artist, distinguishing its parts and demonstrating all. The third introduces the artist to the means and the end, the ability and the desire of acquiring perfect skill and knowledge in painting. May it please you, then, to read me with diligence. If anything here seems to you to need emending, correct me. There was never a writer so learned to whom erudite friends were not useful. I in particular desire to be corrected by you in order not to be pecked at by detractors.

[1] [Donatello, Ghiberti, Luca della Robbia, Masaccio.—Ed.]

Giovanni Rucellai (1403–1481)
Tribute to Brunelleschi,
in *Collected Writings*
(*Zibaldone*) (ca. 1457)

In our city of Florence there were at this time[1] four citizens, prominent and great men [Palla Strozzi, Cosimo de' Medici, Leonardo Bruni, and Filippo Brunelleschi] who were worthy of fame and of immortality. . . .

Filippo di Ser Brunellescho, of whom it is said that from the time the Roman lords ruled the world until now there never was a man more singular in architecture than he, supreme in geometry and a perfect master of sculpture; and in similar things he had very great ingenuity and imagination, and the ancient building art of the Romans was rediscovered by him.

Translated from "Il Zibaldone Quaresimale," in *Giovanni Rucellai ed il suo Zibaldone*, ed. A. Perosa (London, 1960), pp. 54f. See also *Zibaldone*, p. 157, n. 34.

---

[1] [This passage refers to an earlier period (1430s) and is a brief *excursus* which Rucellai inserted into his chronicle of Florentine events of the 1450s.—Ed.]

Anonymous Poet

Stanzas in Praise of Brunelleschi (1459)

He was the master among architects
Who had in that art true wisdom
No one was more exceptional than this man

He vaulted without armature the Cupola
Of the beautiful temple of Santa Maria del Fiore
That is as tall as a great mountain

Even if a body is dead fame does not die
Not that of Filippo di ser Brunellescho
Nor will it ever die until the end of time.

The poem was written in praise of Cosimo de' Medici and the celebration held in Florence in 1459 to honor two distinguished visitors to the city, Pope Pius II and Galeazzo Maria Sforza, son of the Duke of Milan. The Italian text of this portion of the poem is found in C. v. Fabriczy, "Brunelleschiana," *Jahrbuch der Preuszischen Kunstsammlungen,* 28 (1907), *Beiheft,* 40.

Cristoforo Landino (1424–1492)
Appreciation of Brunelleschi, in
*Commentary on the Divine
Comedy of Dante* (1481)

Filippo di Ser Brunellesco was worthy in architecture as well as in painting and sculpture: above all he fully understood perspective and some affirm him to have been its rediscover or inventor: and in one art and the other there are excellent things made by him.

The Italian text of this excerpt from Landino's Introduction to his Commentary on Dante's Divine Comedy is found in O. Morisani, "Art Historians and Art Critics—III, Cristoforo Landino," *Burlington Magazine,* 95 (1953), 270.

Mariano di Jacopo Jaccola
(1382–ca.1454)
From a Record of a Speech
by Brunelleschi (1420s)

Pippo Brunelleschi of the great and mighty city of Florence, a singularly honored man, famous in several arts, gifted by God especially

The footnotes and the translation of the text are reprinted from *Brunelleschi, Studies of His Technology and Inventions,* pp. 128f., by Frank D. Prager and Gustina Scaglia, by permission of the M.I.T. Press, Cambridge, Massachusetts. Copyright © 1970 The Massachusetts Institute of Technology. See also Prager and Scaglia, pp. 125ff.

in architecture, a most learned inventor of devices in mechanics, was kind enough to speak to me in Siena, using these words:[1] Do not share your inventions with many, share them only with few who understand and love the sciences. To disclose too much of one's inventions and achievements is one and the same thing as to give up the fruit of one's ingenuity. Many are ready, when listening to the inventor, to belittle and deny his achievements, so that he will no longer be heard in honorable places, but after some months or a year they use the inventor's words, in speech or writing or design. They boldly call themselves the inventors of the things that they first condemned, and attribute the glory of another to themselves.[2] There is also the great big ingenious fellow, who, having heard of some innovation or invention never known before, will find the inventor and his idea most surprising and ridiculous. He tells him: Go away, do me the favor and say no such things any more—you will be esteemed *a beast*.[3] Therefore the gifts given to us by God must not be relinquished to those who speak ill of them and who are moved by envy or ignorance. We must do that which wise men esteem to be the wisdom of the strong and ingenious:

We must not show to all and sundry the secrets of the waters flowing in ocean and river, or the devices that work on these waters. Let there be convened a council of experts and masters in mechanical art to deliberate what is needed to compose and construct these works. Every person wishes to know of the proposals, the learned and the ignorant; the learned understands the work proposed—he understands at least something, partly or fully—but the ignorant and inexperienced understand nothing, not even when things are explained to them. Their ignorance moves them promptly to anger; they remain in their ignorance because they want to show themselves learned, which they are not, and they move the other ignorant crowd to insistence on its own poor ways and to scorn for those who know. Therefore the *blockheads* and ignorants are a great danger for the aque-

[1] The statement following here may be the only utterance orally made by Brunelleschi that was literally transmitted by a direct witness. Of course, Taccola translates it into his notarial Latin. Words in italics indicate Taccola's use of Italian within his Latin text.
[2] An apparent reference to the debates with Lorenzo Ghiberti.
[3] Brunelleschi seems to paraphrase Acquettini's sonnet. [See below, p. 32. —Ed.]

ducts, the means for forcing the waters, their ascending and descending both subterranean and terrestrial, and the building in water and over the water, be it salt or fresh. Those who know these things are much to be loved, but those who do not are even more to be avoided, and the *headstrong* ignorant should be sent to war. Only the wise should form a council, since they are the honor and glory of the republic. Amen.

Giovanni di Gherardo da Prato,
called Acquettini (1367–ca.1444)

Sonnet Written to Brunelleschi
(ca. 1425)

O you deep fountain, pit of ignorance,
   You miserable beast and imbecile,
   Who thinks uncertain things can be made visible:
   There is no substance to your alchemy.
The fickle mob, eternally deceived
   In all its hope, may still believe in you,
   But never will you, worthless nobody,
   Make that come true which is impossible.
So if the Badalon, your water bird,[1]
   Were ever finished—which can never be—

The translations of Acquettini's sonnet and the response by Brunelleschi are reprinted from *Brunelleschi, Studies of His Technology and Inventions*, p. 118, by Frank D. Prager and Gustina Scaglia, per permission of the M.I.T. Press, Cambridge, Massachusetts. Copyright © 1970 The Massachusetts Institute of Technology. For the Italian texts see Prager and Scaglia, pp. 143f.

---

[1] [The reference is to a transport ship invented by Brunelleschi. See Prager and Scaglia, pp. 111ff.—Ed.]

I would no longer read on Dante at school [2]
But finish my existence with my hand.
For surely you are mad. You hardly know
Your own profession. Leave us, please, alone.

[2] [The author lectured on Dante at the University of Florence.—Ed.]

Filippo Brunelleschi (1377–1446)
Sonnet in Response to Giovanni
di Gherardo da Prato

When hope is given us by Heaven,
O you ridiculous-looking beast,
We rise above corruptible matter
And gain the strength of clearest sight.
A fool will lose what hope he has,
For all experience disappoints him.
For wise men nothing that exists
Remains unseen; they do not share
The idle dreams of would-be scholars.
Only the artist, not the fool
Discovers that which nature hides.
Therefore untangle the web of your verses,
Lest they strike sour notes in the dance
When your "impossible" comes to pass.

Overseers of the Works of
Florence Cathedral

Brunelleschi's Release from
Imprisonment (1434)

AUGUST 20, 1434

The overseers of the Cathedral Works considering [the actions
of] the consuls of the Stonemasons' and Woodworkers' Guild of the
city of Florence—that Filippo [Brunelleschi] has been imprisoned for
not fulfilling an obligation according to the rules of their office;[1] that
they [the consuls] have imprisoned Filippo unjustly and unduly on
the grounds that he designed and built the great Cupola and has not
paid the annual fee to the guild thus dishonoring and disgracing their
authority, and they have done this in order that their authority might
not be mocked—have advised that the Purveyor, Supervisor, and
Notary of the Cathedral Works see to it as quickly as possible that
the consuls of the guild be seized and put in the keeping of one of
the magistrates of Florence at [the overseers'] urgent demand, and
that the consuls not be released without their releasing Filippo.

AUGUST 26, 1434

[The overseers of the Cathedral Works] have deliberated that
the Captain of the People [police magistrate] of the city of Florence

---

The Latin texts of the three documents are found in Guasti, *Cupola,* 1857, p. 54,
docs. 116, 117, 118. Translations by Joan Monahan.

[1] [Members of the Stonemasons' and Woodworkers' Guild were offended that
Brunelleschi, a member of the Silk Guild to which goldsmiths traditionally belonged, had been chosen to construct the Cupola of the Cathedral but did not
matriculate in their Guild and pay its annual fee.—Ed.]

be exhorted to detain in his palace, at their urgent demand, a consul [one Rinaldo di Silvestro] of the [Stonemasons' and Woodworkers'] Guild, and that he not be released without their freeing Filippo. This is to be done in return for the action of the guild against Filippo Brunelleschi and to satisfy the authority of the Cathedral overseers.

AUGUST 31, 1434

[The overseers of the Cathedral Works] have deliberated that Rinaldo di Silvestro, consul of the [Stonemasons' and Woodworkers'] Guild, be released with favor and good will from his imprisonment under the authority of the Captain of the People to the satisfaction of the overseers, since the consuls of the guild have released Filippo Brunelleschi from his imprisonment under the authority of the Court of Appeal.

Andrea di Lazzaro Cavalcanti,
called Il Buggiano (1412–1462)
Expressions of Loyalty
to Brunelleschi

I have no home or property in Florence or father or mother, and two brothers were killed in the war. All the property I have are 200 florins

---

Excerpts from Andrea di Lazzaro Cavalcanti's tax reports in 1433 and, following the death of Brunelleschi, in 1446. The Italian texts are found in C. v. Fabriczy, *Filippo Brunelleschi, Sein Leben und Seine Werke* (Stuttgart, 1892), pp. 522, 524ff.

earned from Filippo di ser Brunelleschi for work that I made. . . . I have been with him for sixteen years.

This is my property, subtracted from the settlement of the will [of Brunelleschi] and all other expenses; I beg that you will recognize that I, Andrea, am a poor boy, brought up by Filippo, and my only desire is to do honor to his good memory [by carving his tombstone at my own expense]. . . .

Pope Eugenius IV (reigned 1431–1447)

Letter on Behalf of Brunelleschi to the Queen of Naples and Sicily (October 23, 1434)

Dearest daughter in Christ, Johanna,[1] honored Queen of Sicily.

Dearest daughter in Christ, greetings and apostolic blessings. Our esteemed son Filippo Brunelleschi, a Florentine citizen, has reared from childhood for fifteen [*sic*] years a certain Andrea di Lazzaro Buggiano in whom he had confidence as in a son. Recently, as he [Brunelleschi] maintains, [Buggiano] took a certain amount of money and some jewels which he [Brunelleschi] entrusted to him as if to a son. After having done so [Buggiano] fled and finally came to Naples where he is said to be at present. Therefore We beseech Your

---

The Latin text is found in C. v. Fabriczy, "Brunelleschiana," *Jahrbuch der Preuszischen Kunstsammlungen,* 28 (1907), *Beiheft,* 80f. Translated by Joan Monahan.

---

[1] [Johanna (Giovanna) II, b. 1371, reigned 1414–1435, descendant of Charles II of Anjou.—Ed.]

Highness that Filippo himself or whomever else he sends for the recovery of this money and jewels be especially recommended to the favor of your help in seeing that justice be administered to them whether it be in Naples or elsewhere in your realm. Indeed We will be pleased with any assistance Your Highness will have extended to this Filippo and his agents for the recovery of these stolen articles. Written at Florence, twenty-third day of October, in the fourth year of Our pontificate [1434].

Lorenzo Ghiberti (*1378–1455*)
The Contest for the Baptistery Door

In my youth in the year of Christ 1400, I left Florence because the air was corrupt and the city in a bad state. I left in the company of a distinguished painter who had been summoned by the Lord Malatesta of Pesaro. He had had a room made which we painted for him with the greatest diligence. . . . At this time however my friends in Florence wrote to me that the governors of the temple of S. Giovanni Battista were sending for skilled masters of whose work they wished to see proof. From all over Italy many skilled masters came to enter this trial and contest. I requested leave from the lord [Malatesta] and from my companion. When the lord [Malatesta] heard the situation he immediately granted me leave; together with other sculptors I went before the committee [of S. Giovanni Battista]. To each one were given four bronze tablets. As the trial piece the committee and the governors of that temple wanted each of us to make one narrative panel for the door. The story they selected was the Sacrifice of Isaac, and each of the contestants had to make the same story. The trial pieces were to be executed in one year and he who

From Ghiberti's *Commentaries* (1447–1448). The Italian text is found in Lorenzo Ghiberti, *I Commentarii,* ed. O. Morisani (Naples, 1947), p. 42.

won would be given the prize. The contestants were these: Filippo di ser Brunellesco, Simone da Colle, Nicolò d'Arezzo, Jacopo della Quercia of Siena, Francesco di Valdambrina, Nicolò Lamberti. There were six[1] taking part in this contest, which was a demonstration of the various aspects of the art of sculpture. To me was conceded the palm of victory by all the experts and by all those who competed with me. Universally I was conceded the glory without exception. At that time it seemed to all, after great consultation and examination by the learned men, that I had surpassed all the others without any exception. The committee of the governors wanted the opinion of the experts written by their own hand. They were highly skilled men among painters, goldsmiths, silversmiths, and marble sculptors. There were thirty-four judges from the city and other places nearby. From all came the declaration of the victory in my favor by the consuls and the committee and the entire body of the Merchants' Guild which is in charge of the temple of S. Giovanni. It was conceded to me and determined that I should make the bronze door for this temple. This I carried out with great diligence. . . .

[1] [Ghiberti neglected to include himself in the count; there were seven contestants. —Ed.]

Antonio di Tuccio Manetti
(1423–1497)
The Contest for the Baptistery Door

In the year of Our Lord 1401 when [Brunelleschi—Ed.] was a young man of twenty-four, working at the goldsmith's art, the *operai*

From *The Life of Brunelleschi* by Antonio di Tuccio Manetti, pp. 46, 48, 50. Introduction, Notes, and Critical Text Edition by Howard Saalman. English translation by Catherine Enggass. Published by the Pennsylvania State University Press, University Park and London. Copyright © 1970 by The Pennsylvania State University. Reprinted by permission.

of the building of the temple of San Giovanni had to commission the making of the second bronze doors (which are today on the north façade) for the embellishment of the aforesaid church. While considering the reputation of the masters of figure casting—including the Florentine masters—in order to assign them to the one who was best, they decided, after many discussions amongst themselves and after counsels with the citizens and artisans, that the two finest they could find were both Florentines and that neither in Florence or elsewhere did they know of anyone better. Those two were the aforementioned Filippo and Lorenzo di Bartolo. The latter's name is inscribed on the doors as Lorenzo di Cione Ghiberti as he was the son of Cione. At the outset of this affair of the doors Lorenzo was a young man also. He was in Rimini in the service of Signor Malatesta when he was called to Florence for this event. The following method was employed to choose the best one: they selected the shape of one of the compartments from the bronze doors that had been made by non-Florentine masters in the last century (although the design of the wax modeled figures was by the painter Giotto) containing the story of St. John. Each of them was given a scene to sculpt in bronze within such a form with the principal intention of commissioning the doors to the one who came out the best in the aforesaid test.

They made those scenes and they have been preserved to this day. The one in the Audience Hall of the Guild of the Merchants is by Lorenzo and the one in the dossal of the sacristy altar of San Lorenzo in Florence is by Filippo. The subject of both is Abraham sacrificing his son. Filippo sculpted his scene in the way that still may be seen today. He made it quickly, as he had a powerful command of the art. Having cast, cleaned, and polished it completely he was not eager to talk about it with anyone, since, as I have said, he was not boastful. He waited for the time of confrontation. It was said that Lorenzo was rather apprehensive about Filippo's merit as [the latter] was very apparent. Since it did not seem to him that he possessed such mastery of the art, he worked slowly. Having been told something of the beauty of Filippo's work he had the idea, as he was a shrewd person, of proceeding by means of hard work and by humbling himself through seeking the counsel—so that his work would not fail at the confrontation—of all the people he esteemed who, being goldsmiths, painters, sculptors, etc. and knowledgeable men, had to do the judging. While making [his scene] in wax he conferred and—humbling himself a great deal—asked for advice constantly of people of that sort and, insofar as he could, he tried to find out how Filippo's work was coming along. He unmade and remade the whole and sections of it without sparing effort, just as often as the majority of the experts in discussing it judged that he should. The *operai* and officials of the church were advised by the very people Lorenzo had singled out. They were in fact the best informed and had been around Lorenzo's work many times: perhaps there was no one else [to consult].

Since none of them had seen Filippo's model they all believed that Polycletus—not to mention Filippo—could not have done better [than Lorenzo]. Filippo's fame was not yet widespread as he was a young man and his mind was fixed on deeds rather than on appearances. However, when they saw his work they were all astonished and marveled at the problems that he had set himself: the attitude, the position of the finger under the chin, and the energy of Abraham; the clothing, bearing, and delicacy of the son's entire figure; the angel's robes, bearing, and gestures and the manner in which he grasps the hand; the attitude, bearing, and delicacy of the figure removing a thorn from his foot and the figure bending over to drink— how complex these figures are and how well they fulfill their functions (there is not a limb that is not alive); the types and the fineness of the animals as well as all the other elements and the composition of the scene as a whole.

Those deputized to do the judging changed their opinion when they saw it. However, it seemed unfeasible to recant what they had said so persistently to anyone who would listen to them, though it now seemed laughable, even though they recognized the truth. Gathering together again they came to a decision and made the following report to the *operai:* both models were very beautiful and for their part, taking everything into consideration, they were unable to put one ahead of the other, and since it was a big undertaking requiring much time and expense they should commission it to both equally and they should be partners. When Filippo and Lorenzo were summoned and informed of the decision, Lorenzo remained silent while Filippo was unwilling to consent unless he was given entire charge of the work. On that point he was unyielding. The officials made the decision thinking that certainly they would in the end agree. Filippo, like one who unknowingly has been destined for some greater tasks by God, refused to budge. The officials threatened to assign it to Lorenzo if he did not change his mind: he answered that he wanted no part of it if he did not have complete control, and if they were unwilling to grant it they could give it to Lorenzo as far as he was concerned. With that they made their decision. Public opinion in the city was completely divided as a result. Those who took Filippo's side were very displeased that the commission for the whole work had not been given to him. However, that is what happened, and in view of what was awaiting Filippo experience proved that it was for the best.

Giorgio Vasari (1511–1574)

The Contest for the Baptistery Door

In the year 1401, it was proposed to make the two bronze doors of the church and baptistery of S. Giovanni, sculpture having advanced so greatly, because from the time of the death of Andrea Pisano there had not been any masters capable of carrying them out. Accordingly this purpose was made known to the sculptors then in Tuscany, who were invited to come, provided with maintenance and set to prepare a panel. Among those thus invited were Filippo and Donato, Lorenzo Ghiberti, Jacopo della Fonte, Simone da Colle, Francesco di Valdambrina and Niccolo d' Arezzo.[1] The panels were completed that same year, and when they came to be exhibited in

From the book *Lives of the Painters, Sculptors and Architects* by Giorgio Vasari. Ed. by Wm. Grant. Trans. by A. B. Hinds. Everyman's Library Edition. Published by E. P. Dutton & Co., Inc., New York, and J. M. Dent & Sons Ltd., London, and used with their permission. Vol. I., pp. 273f.

[1] [See below, p. 46, n5. —Ed.]

competition they were all most beautiful, each different from the other. That of Donato was well designed and badly executed; that of Jacopo della Quercia was well designed and executed, but with faulty perspective of the figures; that of Francesco di Valdambrina had poor invention and tiny figures; the worst of all were those of Niccolo d' Arezzo and Simone da Colle, and the best that of Lorenzo di Ghiberti, combining design, diligence, invention and art, the figures being beautifully made. Not much inferior to his, however, was the panel of Filippo, on which he had represented Abraham sacrificing Isaac, with a servant extracting a thorn from his foot while waiting for Abraham, and an ass grazing, which merits considerable praise. When the scenes came to be exhibited, Filippo and Donato were only satisfied with that of Lorenzo, judging it to be better adapted to its peculiar purpose than those of the others. So they persuaded the consuls with good arguments that the work should be given to Lorenzo, showing that both public and private ends would be best served thereby. This was a true act of friendship, a virtue without envy, and a clear judgment of their own limitations, so that they deserve more praise than if they had completed that work themselves. Happy spirits who, while assisting each other, rejoice in praising the work of others! How unhappy are the men of our own times, who try to injure others, and burst with envy if they cannot vent their malice. Filippo was requested by the consuls to undertake the work together with Lorenzo, but he refused, as he preferred to be the first in another art, rather than be equal or second in that.

Richard Krautheimer

The Contest for the Baptistery Door

. . . The *Commentarii* and the *Vita di Brunellesco* concur on
the date of 1401 for the opening of the competition, and Ghiberti's
description of the proceedings corresponds by and large with what
apparently became standard procedure thirty years later. . . . The
committee which the *Calimala* [Merchants' Guild] had put in charge
of the Baptistery, the *Officiali del Musaico* or as it was popularly
called the *Operai* or *Governatori*,[1] very likely set up the general conditions of the contest, presumedly with the approval of the consuls of
the guild, and allotted the funds necessary for the occasion. To assure
themselves of having a competent master they decided to announce a
contest, inviting "skilled masters from all the lands of Italy" to participate. In order to prepare for and supervise the competition properly, the *Officiali del Musaico* held a consultation with an advisory jury
of thirty-four members on questions of technical and artistic conduct.
The committee must have been responsible for the rules of the contest and obviously determined the general scheme of the door which
in the end was to be commissioned to the winner as an award: like
Andrea's, it was to be divided into twenty-eight panels, each a
braccio wide and containing a quatrefoil. The committee selected the
general subject matter and possibly, though not necessarily, deter-

Selections from Chapter III, "The Competition" (with cuts), and Chapter IV, "The
Competition Reliefs: Ghiberti and Brunelleschi," in Richard Krautheimer and
Trude Krautheimer-Hess, *Lorenzo Ghiberti,* Reissue (copyright © 1970 by Princeton University Press), Vol. I, pp. 36–43, 44–49. Reprinted by permission of Princeton University Press. Bibliography cited in footnotes appears immediately following
these selections.

[1] Ghiberti himself uses the term *operai di detto governo;* see Ghiberti-Schlosser,
bibl. 178, i, p. 46.

mined the sequence of scenes and individual figures thereof. Certainly it was the committee that decided upon the subject for the competition panel and set the deadline for its completion.

The competition, proceeding by and large along these lines, was not without its difficulties. During the contest or shortly thereafter, just before work began, the program of the door was changed. At the commencement of the competition, the projected subject matter was the Old Testament; Ghiberti writes that the committee insisted on making every competitor design "one story of this door . . . the Sacrifice of Isaac." Later, "it was decided to place the New Testament on this door" and to save the prize-winning relief of the Sacrifice of Isaac "for the other door, if there the Old Testament should be represented." . . .

Since a cycle of the Old Testament was planned, the choice of the competition panel obviously had to be a scene common to Old Testament cycles, for it would only be sensible to incorporate the winning relief into the final scheme. The Sacrifice of Isaac was the outstanding typological prefiguration of the Crucifixion and as such formed throughout the Middle Ages part and parcel of all large Old Testament cycles. To choose this theme for the competition was then the natural thing to do.

But the committee of the *Operai,* instead of simply prescribing this subject, apparently went further and drew up a specific set of requirements; for it can hardly be by chance that the competition reliefs of both Brunelleschi and Ghiberti contain the same number of figures and exceed the limits of the Sacrifice proper. Alongside the traditional elements of the subject—Abraham, Isaac, the angel appearing from heaven, the ram and thicket—there are two servants at the foot of the rock and an ass drinking from the fountain. The appearance of this particular combination of figures in both reliefs is so remarkable a coincidence as strongly to suggest that the committee of the *Calimala* requested it. The combination is not traditional. As a rule, the Sacrifice and the waiting servants form two different scenes as, indeed, they are described in Genesis 22.[2]

---

[2] Throughout the Middle Ages scenes of the Sacrifice were limited to the principal actors: Isaac kneels on the altar; Abraham lifts the sword; the hand of God or of an angel appears from heaven; and the ram is hidden in the bush. Such scenes appear first in fourth century sarcophagi and pyxides and continue as late as

. . . The committee in charge of the contest apparently selected the participants as well. The sources, in truth, disagree somewhat on the procedure used here. The *Vita di Brunellesco* maintains that only Brunelleschi and Ghiberti were asked to compete, but this assertion was obviously dictated by a desire to single out Florence as the most important city of the time.[3] Ghiberti, in the *Commentarii*, likewise suggests that the competitors were chosen by invitation of the committee, who "sent for masters who should be skilled and of whose work they wanted to see proof," but evidently additional candidates, like Ghiberti himself, could also apply at the suggestion of "friends in Florence."[4] The first large group may have been narrowed down by the committee; in any case, the final run included only seven: Filippo di Ser Brunellesco, Simone da Colle, Niccolo di Luca Spinelli, known as Niccolo d'Arezzo, Jacopo della Quercia, Francesco di Valdambrino, Niccolo di Piero Lamberti and Lorenzo Ghiberti.[5] It was a most

---

the thirteenth and fourteenth centuries, represented in the *Psalter of Saint Louis* (Paris, Bibl. Nat., lat. 10525; Omont, bibl. 373, pl. x), in Torriti's fresco in Assisi (Van Marle, bibl. 301, I, fig. 109) and in Giusto da Menabuoi's frescoes in Padua. Throughout medieval art the ass and servants seem never to be shown in the same scene as the Sacrifice proper; they are accessories, fully developed or abbreviated, but always distinct from the main scene. In the ninth century *Cosmas Indicopleustes* the servants are shown walking with the ass, led by Abraham and Isaac, the latter carrying the fagot (Vat. Gr. 699, f. 59; Stornaiolo, bibl. 507, pl. 22); in another scene on this page the Sacrifice is represented. At about the same time (880–886) the *Homilies of Gregory of Nazianz* (Paris, Bibl. Nat., gr. 510, f. 174; Omont, bibl. 372, pl. 37) shows Abraham bidding the servants to wait with their beast of burden, while Isaac with the fagot precedes him up the hill; the Sacrifice as always is depicted in another scene. The two scenes remain clearly separated until the High and Late Middle Ages. In the *Bible of Jean de Sy, ca.* 1356 (Paris, Bibl. Nat., fr. 15397) Abraham is shown bidding the servants to wait; on f. 36v they wait, while their ass drinks from the fountain and Abraham and Isaac ascend the mountain (Martin, bibl. 306, fig. LXI, pl. 45; fig. LXII, pl. 46). Usually Isaac carries the fagot (Franco-Flemish Bible, Lille, Witter Coll., late thirteenth century; psalter of Queen Isabeau, Munich, Staatsbibliothek, gall. 16, f. 29v; a French psalter, fourteenth century, Oxford, Bodl., Auct. D. 44; James, bibl. 230, pl. 27b). Needless to say, this motif serves as a typological parallel to Christ bearing the Cross in the *Biblia Pauperum* and the *Speculum Humanae Salvationis* of the late Middle Ages (Cornell, bibl. 106 *passim;* Lutz-Perdrizet, bibl. 284, pp. 170, 214; bibl. 43).

[3] (Manetti), bibl. 294, p. 14.
[4] Ghiberti-Schlosser, bibl. 178, I, pp. 45f.
[5] The most recent and authoritative monograph on Quercia is Bacci's, bibl. 31. Bacci has also published the only monograph in existence on Francesco da Val-

remarkable selection. The origin of the contestants, their age and training, were probably all discussed and criticized by committee and outsiders alike, and such criticism is, indeed, reflected in the *Vita di Brunellesco*. The contest was not limited to Florentines and although the seven were not "from all over Italy," they did come from various parts of Tuscany. Only two, Brunelleschi and Ghiberti, were sons of Florentine citizens. One, Simone da Colle, was from the old Florentine territory of Val d'Elsa. Niccolo Lamberti, though settled in Florence, came from an Aretine family. Niccolo di Luca Spinelli apparently resided in Arezzo which, just sixteen years before, had been purchased by the republic of Florence, thus making Spinelli a Florentine subject, but not a citizen. The group was further broadened by the admittance of two artists, Jacopo della Quercia and Francesco da Valdambrino, who actually came from the old arch enemy of Florence, Siena. Florentine *campanilismo* must have winced. The disparity of age between the competitors was no doubt a point for an issue of much argument. Except for Niccolo di Luca Spinelli, apparently about fifty, and Jacopo della Quercia, about forty, all were young. Niccolo di Piero Lamberti was just over thirty and Francesco da Valdambrino about the same. Brunelleschi and Ghiberti were the youngest, twenty-three and about twenty respectively. Diversity of training among the contestants must also have led to objections: Niccolo d'Arezzo and Brunelleschi were in good standing as goldsmiths; Simone da Colle later gained fame as a cannon founder; Quercia and Francesco da Valdambrino were sculptors and woodcarvers together with Niccolo di Piero Lamberti, another respected member of the guild for woodcarvers and stonecutters; young Ghiberti, though probably trained as a goldsmith, up until then had worked only as a painter.

The outcome of the competition is known. Late in 1402, *stile fiorentino*, that is prior to March 25, 1403, one and a half or two years after its opening, the consuls of the *Calimala* decided to entrust the execution of the door to Ghiberti, the youngest competitor. . . .

---

dambrino, bibl. 30. The identities of Niccolo Lamberti and Niccolo di Luca Spinelli have been definitely established by Procacci, bibl. 427, pp. 300ff. Thus, the personality of only one of the competitors, Simone da Colle, remains obscure.

Vasari (Vasari-Milanesi, bibl. 533, II, pp. 226, 335) adds to this list of competitors the name of Donatello, quite arbitrarily it would seem. The date of his birth, probably 1386, precludes his participation.

Shortly afterwards, prior to March 1403, a first payment of 30 florins was made to "Nencio di Bartoluccio" [Ghiberti—Ed.] possibly for the purchase of the competition relief and for the gilding. . . . The decision of the consuls was apparently based on a report drawn up by the *Operai* and this in turn rested upon a written declaration requested by them of the jury "the committee of regents wanted their [the experts'] judgment written in their own hand." Yet it appears that the consuls also invited the opinion of rank and file members of the guild, for Ghiberti explicitly states that everyone approved his victory, "consuls and *Operai* and the entire body of the *Arte Mercatoria*." The procedure seems unusual, but then Ghiberti's words can hardly be disregarded.[6]

It is understandable that the committee of regents, the *Operai*, may have wanted to protect its final actions by a written declaration as evidence of the jury's verdict. The jury of experts was composed of persons as diverse in training and origin as the seven contestants, being "painters, gold and silversmiths and sculptors . . . from the city and other neighboring places." Yet despite all the precautions taken to arrive at a disinterested verdict, the situation remained delicate and to have the judgment down in black and white could do no harm. Already the choice of the final seven, many of them young and not even trained as metal workers, had been open to attack. Now the first prize fell to the youngest of all, a lad of twenty, and, worse, he was not a member of the goldsmiths' or sculptors' guilds; it is not even certain that he was matriculated in the *Medici e Spetiali*, the guild in which, as a painter, he should have enrolled. Most shocking of all, he was not yet a master. Brunelleschi, but a few years his senior, had by 1398 applied for registration as a goldsmith and could expect to matriculate as a master simply by payment of a few florins, as indeed he did in 1404.[7] Ghiberti on the other hand, had to work in the name of the firm of his stepfather, Bartolo di Michele; if a contract were signed, it had to be worded in such a way as to make Bartoluccio, as a master of good standing in the *Arte della Seta*, undertake legal responsibility. A situation of this sort was almost certain to give rise to accusations of unfairness, preferential treatment, and discrimination.

[6] Ghiberti-Schlosser, bibl. 178, I, p. 46; II, pp. 168ff.
[7] *ASF, Arti, Seta, Matricola*, vol. VII, c.68v; quoted by Fabriczy, bibl. 148, p. 5.

In fact, there is more than just slight evidence of accusations of this kind. By the time Ghiberti wrote his *Commentarii,* forty years later, such recriminations may have been more vocal and they became rampant in the *Vita di Brunellesco.* Of course, the particulars, as the *Vita* handles them, are distorted. Filippo is constantly presented as the young independent genius who went about his task disdaining favors and asking advice from no one. Ghiberti, on the other hand, is accused of scheming, underhanded methods such as apple-polishing the jury by asking their advice and remodeling his relief in response to their suggestions. But, according to the *Vita,* despite all Ghiberti's maneuvers, the experts turned in a report which appointed first prize to both Ghiberti and Brunelleschi. They were asked to design and cast the door jointly and only because Brunelleschi refused to share the honor was Ghiberti left the sole victor.[8] Studio Gossip in Florence in the last quarter of the century clearly persisted in the rumor that at the time of the contest opinion had been sharply divided. Perhaps such gossip did not arise before the thirties or forties. The bronze door which Ghiberti executed as a result of his triumph, while still admired by laymen, was then considered by *cognoscenti* obsolete and far surpassed by the new door, the Gates of Paradise. In this Ghiberti himself agreed by implication with the younger generation, the leaders of the *Calimala,* who in 1452 moved his first door to the less conspicuous North Gate. Brunelleschi, meanwhile, had achieved the difficult feat of vaulting the dome of the Cathedral, the pride of all Florentines, and had set up all over town buildings in a new and bold style, thus earning himself the status of the grand old man of modern architecture. His early defeat in the competition had somehow to be satisfactorily explained away, a wish and sentiment all too clearly reflected in the *Vita.*

Yet, the fact that opinion was later divided does not preclude the possibility that dissension existed at the time of the competition, dissension which only grew more bitter with time. It is sharply brought out in the *Vita di Brunellesco* that even in 1420 "the city still smelled from the bile of the bronze doors" (la città teneva dello umore delle porte del bronzo). Ghiberti himself, in discussing the contest in the *Commentarii* shortly before 1450, seems rather anxious to justify the

[8] (Manetti), bibl. 294, p. 42.

final judgment in his favor. He is insistent about the fact that the opinion of the jury was declared in writing and puts great stress on the agreement reached by all ranks of the *Calimala* as to his worthiness, repeating three times in succession that the jury, the officials of the guild, the rank and file and "even those who competed against me" [9] were unanimously in his favor. He underscores the differences among the judges in background and profession. All this reiteration betrays a sense of uneasiness on the old master's part, undoubtedly aroused by some clash of opinion in wider art circles. His qualifying phrase, "at that time," meaning that he received unanimous approval at the time of the competition, suggests that when writing the *Commentarii* he was aware of and resented a growing opposition to his early work.

Several scraps of evidence, circumstantial it is true, tend to support the claim that the competition once ended in a tie. In the first place, the precautions taken by the various organs of the *Calimala* in order to justify their final choice seem quite extraordinary. It was unprecedented to secure a written declaration of opinion from the jury and furthermore to take recourse in the opinions of the rank and file. It would seem that such motions were specially devised on this occasion, so as to give added weight to the final decision. Secondly, of all the reliefs entered in the contest, only two survive, Ghiberti's and Brunelleschi's. . . . [Figs. 3, 4]. Naturally Ghiberti's would be preserved, since it was prize-winner and intended for use in the other door, "if there the Old Testament should be represented." The members of the *Calimala* were, after all, shrewd businessmen who would not be more wasteful than necessary. By the same token, it seems strange that Brunelleschi's competition entry was not melted down as presumably the rest of the losers' were. If his plaque was deliberately saved, despite the sheer waste of seventy-five pounds of good bronze, there must have been a reason for it and the likeliest is that the jury wished to keep it as evidence in support of its own split choice in the final decision.

Ghiberti's relief went to the audience hall of the *Arte di Calimala*; Brunelleschi's, after 1421, was inserted in the back slab of the altar in the Old Sacristy of S. Lorenzo,[10] allegedly presented as a

[9] Ghiberti-Schlosser, bibl. 178, **i**, p. 46.
[10] (Manetti), bibl. 294, p. 15.

gift by the master to Cosimo di Medici. Both plaques entered the Bargello in 1859 by way of the Uffizi. Of the reliefs of the other contestants, nothing is known. Probably none survived and Vasari's vague suggestions to the contrary must be discarded as unreliable. . . .[11]

A division of opinion would seem not only justified but almost forced upon the experts when they were confronted with the reliefs of Ghiberti and Brunelleschi: two artists could hardly be more different in style, technique, personality, and background. Together they vividly illuminate the divergent artistic trends in Florence at the beginning of the fifteenth century. Opinions were bound to clash among the members of the jury and their disagreement no doubt had repercussions in talk all over town.[12]

Brunelleschi approaches the Abraham and Isaac story with dramatic force. . . . [Fig. 3] He divides the plaque horizontally into two registers. In the upper, much larger tier, Abraham rushes from the right towards Isaac. The boy kneels on the altar, his right leg forward, his head bent back, his body moving quickly away from the threatening knife. The father's left hand presses Isaac's chin upwards to free his throat for the blow; the knife, in his right hand, is touching the boy's skin. But the angel rushes down from a massive cloud on the left; his left arm shoots forth to grab Abraham's wrist,

---

[11] In his first edition Vasari says only that Ghiberti's and Brunelleschi's reliefs were the best, Donatello's good, Quercia's on a par with Donatello's and Francesco's, Simone's and Niccolo's the worst (Vasari-Ricci, bibl. 531, I, p. 261). In the second edition he elaborates on this statement (Vasari-Milanesi, bibl. 533, II, p. 226), going so far as to say that Donatello's relief had been given to the *Arte del Cambio*, and thereby intimating that he, Vasari, was acquainted with it (Vasari-Milanesi, bibl. 533, II, p. 335). But he clearly never saw such a relief and, indeed, omits any mention of it in Donatello's Vita (*ibid.*, II, pp. 395ff). Scattered throughout the Vite of Ghiberti, Brunelleschi, Quercia, and Niccolo d'Arezzo, are descriptions of the other competition reliefs, but they are kept general and are obviously based on Vasari's actual or pretended knowledge of the styles of the respective masters (*ibid.*, II, pp. 113, 226f, 335). Probably Vasari was just giving his imagination free rein; see also Ghiberti-Schlosser, bibl. 178, II, p. 169.

An engraving, dating *ca.* 1460–70, of the Sacrifice of Isaac (Uffizi 27) has been believed to reproduce one of the competition panels (Kristeller, bibl. 255, pp. 277ff), but the hypothesis is doubtful, to say the least. See also Hind, bibl. 213, I, p. 27; II, pl. 5, and Ghiberti-Schlosser, bibl. 178, II, p. 170.

[12] Comparisons between Ghiberti's and Brunelleschi's reliefs are legion. We refer only to the most recent one, Shapley-Kennedy, bibl. 492.

forcing it back from Isaac's throat—one feels the resistance of the surprised patriarch. The ram, below the angel, is very much in evidence; so is the cliff to the right behind Abraham, surmounted by a small tree that is almost covered by the fluttering cloak of the old man. Abraham, Isaac, and the ram form what appears to be almost an isosceles triangle. In the lower tier, forming its base, spread across the width of the foreground, are the two servants, one in each corner, utterly unconcerned with the main event. The ass between them drinks from the spring at the right. All the figures are in the round; their draperies are heavy, with deep, massive folds. The faces are strong, with broad planes, crowned by heavy wiglike masses of hair. The figures are set against an empty blank ground, parallel to the front plane, on two superimposed narrow stages. No attempt is made to convey depth within the relief. On the contrary, the two servants in the foreground jut forth frontwise and sideways beyond the frame. The scenery is confined to a few props: a steep, sharply cut cliff, two dwarfed trees with scanty, fan-shaped twigs. Every corner of the plaque is painstakingly filled: the upper left lobe by the angel, the upper right lobe by the cliff, the lower ones each by one of the servants; the left corner of the quatrefoil contains the ram, the right corner, an end of Abraham's mantle and a spur of the cliff, the one at the bottom the donkey's right foreleg. The entire plaque is covered by figures and objects, in a *horror vacui*.

At first glance the relief appears strikingly new and exciting, and a good number of the judges, artists and laymen, must have been impressed. It is the work of a young man, awkward in places. But it is brimming over with the impetuosity and the endless curiosity of youth; it teems with an experimenter's love of difficult problems and intricate solutions. The story is told in the most violent language. Every movement, every detail is designed to impress, every gesture meant to shock. The dramatic force of the narrative and the abundance of realistic detail were bound to arouse admiration. Such admiration is indeed reflected in the *Vita di Brunellesco*. The author praises just those surprising and shocking effects: "that finger under the (victim's) chin;" the angel "how he seizes Abraham's hand," the servant "who pulls a splinter from his foot and the other who bends down to drink." No less impressive to some certainly was the central scene: the gawky boniness of Isaac's adolescent torso, the bent-up toes of both his feet, the muscles and tendons of his thighs and calves, the mouth open in a half-choked cry; Abraham's bald pate surrounded by long disorderly coils of hair, the veins and tendons in his left hand, the uncouth butcher knife, and the flames spitting from the altar. Not even the circumcision of Isaac's membrum is forgotten. The foreground is almost completely filled by the donkey. His legs are far apart, his neck strained towards the fountain, two thin threads of water drip from his mouth. The joints, bones and tendons of his legs and rump are sharply outlined, the short mane shaggy and bristling, the knees of the forelegs are marred by deep roundish scars. A knotted rope dangles from behind his right ear, the saddle is worn through, showing the straw filling; one can almost smell the sweat and dirt of the leather. Likewise the ram scratching an ear with a hindleg must have pleased a public which admired this stark but rather obvious realism in the presentation of a narrative so colorful and exciting in itself.

It is a bold realism, delighting in experiments. The two servants are antithetic studies in movement, body, and drapery. The thornpicker to the left sits straight with only head and shoulders bent, his body barely shown through the heavy cloak, his skull hidden under a rich crop of curls. The servant at the right edge crouches low, his whole body nearly bent double. His jerkin is so tight that it almost bursts at the seams from the violent movement; his shaven head (or is it a leather cap?) brings out the form of his skull. Legs and arms cross and overlap in different combinations in each figure. Isaac kneels, his feet pointing left, his chest *en face*, his head violently turned upward and right.

Brunelleschi, then, sets up, as it were, a series of experiments; he carefully selects a number of positions enabling him to inquire into the nature of movement, the interplay of limbs and body and the relation between body and garment. This spirit of inquiry is the very essence of his design. Various elements borrowed from antiquity, scattered as they are throughout the relief, form part and parcel of this approach. They were used not merely because they were obviously rare tidbits for humanist connoisseurs, but because the figures *all'antica*, seated, kneeling, crouching, bent and double-bent, were bold experiments in, and useful tools for, the study of movement. . . . All this makes a daring and aggressive competition piece; but it does not necessarily make a great piece of sculpture. Indeed, the entire relief is full of strange inconsistencies. Alongside the genuine discovery of reality as a means of forceful artistic expression and antiquity as a tool for its realization, stands a bulky and conservative figure design and composition. Certainly the result proves that the jury did not consider these revolutionary and experimental aspects a decisive factor in their final judgment. Perhaps the majority were more aware of the awkwardness of composition, its somewhat trite plan, the overloading with detail, the incongruencies between traditional types and dramatically new additions. The conservative taste of some jurors may well have been shocked by Brunelleschi's experiments.

The goldsmiths on the jury were probably struck by the technical deficiency of Brunelleschi's competition piece. Instead of casting the relief in one piece, as did Ghiberti, he cast a solid plaque, approximately 5 mm thick and soldered onto it the individual pieces of his composition, cast solid and fastened down with crude pegs for greater safety. One large piece comprises the block of rock in the foreground, the ass and ram to the left, the altar and possibly the body of Isaac,[13] the figure of Abraham, together with the rock behind him and the left hand of the angel. Four smaller, individual pieces are added: the two servants, the angel, and the tree on the rock rising behind Abraham. The rock, again in contrast to Ghiberti, is roughened not by casting but by the traditional method of stippling. This method of casting the relief in several pieces, fastening them onto a solid plaque, must have weighed heavily in the jury's adverse decision, for practical as well as technical reasons. If the entire relief were cast in one hollow sheet, as Ghiberti's was, minor failings could be easily corrected by soldering small pieces onto the back of the relief. But if the figures were cast solid, such corrections would be made impossible.[14] Secondly, Brunelleschi's relief was much heavier than Ghiberti's, 25.5 kg as against 18.5 kg (76% Florentine pounds vs. 55% pounds).[15] The twenty-eight reliefs of the North door, if cast by

[13] Even after repeated rechecking, I am not certain whether the body of Isaac was cast separately or together with this large piece.
[14] I am indebted for this and many other observations on the technique of Ghiberti's works to Cavaliere Bruno Bearzi.
[15] I am most grateful to the *Sopraintendenza ai Monumenti* in Florence and especially to Dr. Filippo Rossi, for giving me permission to take the two competition reliefs off their wooden frames.

Brunelleschi, would thus have required an additional 600 Florentine pounds of bronze. No doubt the *prudentes viri* of the *Calimala* thought twice before agreeing to raise the cost of the reliefs even by roughly 60 florins[16] for additional materials alone. True, within the final overall cost of the door 60 florins made little difference. But in 1402 and 1403 the enormous total cost of 16,000 florins could hardly have been foreseen even by the most far-sighted committee members.

Nothing could be more in contrast to Brunelleschi's relief than Ghiberti's [Fig. 4]. Technically it was infinitely superior. Only the figure of Isaac was cast separately, together with Abraham's left hand and a small piece of the rock underneath; all the rest was cast in one piece, forming a strong sheet of bronze, an average of 9 mm thick, and hollow, save for the solid top, right edges, and lower left lobe of the quatrefoil. Minor failings in the casting had been repaired and weak spots reinforced, notably behind the figure of Isaac and behind the foreleg of the donkey. The lesser weight and the ease with which such recasting could be carried out made Ghiberti's relief the more economical. Also an exceedingly fine job of finishing was done throughout. The tiny flaws in the surface are hardly visible and every detail has been gone over with chisel and file: the faces are worked, down to the smallest wrinkle; the little snail-like curls reveal every strand of hair; Abraham's toes are visible through the stockings, the embroidered details of his garment are clear down to the tiniest twig and flower.

The contrast is equally marked in design and narrative. True, Ghiberti also divides the quatrefoil into two sections corresponding to the two parts of the narrative. But he is careful not to cut it up horizontally into two tiers. Instead, he presents the story in two groups which are both separated and connected by a diagonal rocky ridge running from upper left to lower right. To the left, underneath the rocky dividing line, stand the two servants, looking at each other and talking with reticent gestures across the back of the donkey. To the right, above the ridge, Abraham bends over Isaac. The ram is perched above him high on top of the cliff to the left; the angel floats down from the upper right. The quatrefoil serves merely as a frame; much different from Brunelleschi's, it is not scrupulously filled

[16] The standard price for bronze fluctuated from 6½ to 7 *soldi* per *libra*. . . .

up in all its lobes and corners. The figures fall into clear small groups, separated by scenery. They are set off against rock or placed against carefully balanced stretches of blank ground. The pause, as it were, has been turned into a dynamic feature of creative design.

Also, in contrast to Brunelleschi's design, the groups in Ghiberti's relief do not run parallel to the front plane. Two or three figures are crowded together. They frequently turn into the relief or half out of it in poses that stress three-quarter views, half-lost profiles or movements that twist slightly from one pose to the other. The young servant to the left pivots on his feet; Isaac turns in a clockwise move from right to left, his left thigh facing right, his chest parallel to the picture plane, his head thrown sharply upwards and to the left. Abraham pushes back into the relief with his right hip, only to thrust forward his head, his right arm and his left leg. Within the groups figures face or move in opposite directions, creating "space caves" in which to stand and by which to hint at depth. The space around the group of servants is not identical with that around Abraham and Isaac, nor is either area completely unified within itself. Thus it happens that the top part of the older servant's body protrudes from the rock almost in the round, while his legs are but faintly marked as if much further away. But space is intimated, the back plaque suggesting atmosphere rather than blank ground. The two servants are enclosed in the cavity of the rock. They face each other and in the gap that separates them the donkey thrusts forward, his neck bent and craned. Thus the narrow space to which the figures are confined is filled by a multitude of gestures and movements. An intricate network of directional forces is established. Abraham and Isaac are separated by a deep gap and again space seems an active force spreading out and enveloping the figures of father and son.

Every movement hints at depth. The figures do not, as in Brunelleschi's relief take violent, yet frozen poses: Abraham in a beautifully swaying, almost protective curve, bends over his son and the boy's body follows the curve of his father's stance. The angel above, the cloak below, continue the movement of the patriarch, closing the half circle and completing the rhythm of the group. In a counter-movement, the servants swing out towards the left in a slight curve. Every gesture is sure, yet delicate and nervous. The figures rest lightly on their feet: the young servant drawing one leg back, lifts his heel barely and touches the ground with his toes; Abraham thrusts his leg forward, the knee hardly bent, yet clearly marked through his garment. His arm is tense and muscular, yet incredibly fine. No part, no movement is ever violent. The draperies, thin and light, follow the motions of the figures in long-drawn curves.

Every detail aims at supporting this melodious, yet not prettified beauty. The modeling of the heads is built up from the bone structure; the cheekbones protrude strongly, brows and the foreheads overshadow deep-set eyes. Faces are rendered in small nervous planes, noses thin, and nostrils appearing to vibrate. Small particulars are modeled with the utmost sharpness and precision, but they blend with the entity of the face. Heads dominate bodies, and their movements and glances replace dramatic action. In the torso of Isaac the skin seems silky, the bones are well padded with flesh. Hands and fingers are long and thin, veins and tendons distinct under the skin. Hair throughout is rendered in tiny light and soft curls, including the fur of the ram and the mane of the donkey. Cloaks are richly embroidered along the hems; Abraham's garment is distinguished by two large panels of embroidery running along the chest and skirt. A few long curved folds are raised above the surface, accompanied and countered by a wealth of short, slightly curved intervening grooves. The entire drapery is lively and articulate, whereas in Brunelleschi's design a few strong folds are separated by wide empty gaps. Light and shade flicker over the surface in tempered contrasts of light and dark, with highlights on shoulders, thighs, ribs and arms, on the ridges of the folds in the cloaks, on brows and cheekbones, creating a network of relationships that leads the eye quickly from figure to figure and ties the composition into a perfect, yet lightly held unit.

The narrative, while clearly intelligible, merely hints at the events. It does not present them with brutal directness as does Brunelleschi. Abraham has raised the knife, but hesitates to strike; his left arm is placed lovingly around Isaac's shoulder. The boy looks at his father, full of confidence; the angel floats down leisurely, sure to arrive in good time. The servants, to the left, talk to each other and the older appears to indicate the mountain where the miracle takes place. Although avoiding dramatic gestures, they are not wholly unconcerned like Brunelleschi's waiting servants, but participate from afar as supporting actors in the drama of the Sacrifice, fulfilling a role not unlike the choir in a Greek tragedy. All the participants of the drama communicate with each other by glances and slight gestures. Even the beholder is made to feel at one with them. His eye enters the scene by way of the beckoning back of the young servant. From there it glides easily over the donkey to the older servant and is hence led by his gesture to the main group. From Abraham's head it wanders along his arm to the face of Isaac, then to the angel and finally back down to the servant. The interplay of movements and glances, the psychological differentiations, are incredibly complex. But they are presented with the greatest possible ease.

As one would expect of any work done between the years 1390 and 1410, realistic details heighten the credibility of the scene: the donkey stands with his forelegs apart, drinking from the fountain; its saddle is shabby and worn through like the one in Brunelleschi's relief. Logs are heaped on the altar. A lizard scurries across the rock in the foreground. But such elements are few, employed with reticence. Very much in contrast to Brunelleschi, the conquest of reality through experimentation is not a final aim to Ghiberti. His figures are not set up as studies in movement or in the relation between body and drapery. He does not attempt to take the beholder by surprise, to attract attention by shocking gestures or intricate and intriguing poses. Reality is not signified to him by the extraordinary event or movement, the drama, the loud outcry. Indeed, he strives for credibility rather than for realism: credibility based on the perceptive handling of a face and body, instead of on a few striking movements; on the subtle interplay of glances and gestures rather than on ferocious dramatization. Like Brunelleschi, Ghiberti draws time and again on the art of antiquity. Isaac's torso is taken from an antique; a Roman acanthus scroll fills the front slab of the altar. But none of these motifs sticks out obtrusively. Ghiberti merges all elements into a consistent and unified atmosphere, with no attempt to overwhelm the beholder; he convinces him instead by the very ease and perfect sureness of his presentation.

Ghiberti's relief in its complete mastery of means is of almost uncanny perfection; superbly finished in every detail, a great feat of craftsmanship and in its sureness hardly credible as the work of a young man just past twenty. It lacks the freshness and vehemence of Brunelleschi's relief; it shows none of the love of experiment or the rebellious violence which made Brunelleschi's piece both awkward and intriguing. Yet the very absence of rebellious elements in Ghiberti's relief may have been one of its great virtues in the eyes of part of the jury. The perfect ease of the design, the convincing yet forceful quiet of the composition and narrative and, last not least, its infinitely superior technical perfection were decisive, one would suppose, in obtaining the much coveted award for the young goldsmith Ghiberti.

BIBLIOGRAPHY

30. P. BACCI, *Francesco di Valdambrino,* Siena, 1936.

31. P. BACCI, *Jacopo della Quercia,* Siena, 1929.

106. H. CORNELL, *Biblia Pauperum,* Stockholm, 1925.

148. C. VON FABRICZY, *Filippo Brunelleschi,* Stuttgart, 1892.

178. LORENZO GHIBERTI, *Lorenzo Ghiberti's Denkwuerdigkeiten (I Commentarii),* 2 vols., ed. J. von Schlosser, Berlin, 1912.

213. A. M. HIND, *Early Italian Engraving,* New York and London, 1938.

230. M. R. JAMES, *Illustrations of the Book of Genesis . . . facs. of the Ms. Brit. Mus. Egerton 1894 (Roxburghe Club,* 177), Oxford, 1921.

255. P. KRISTELLER, "Un ricordo della gara per le porte del Battistero di Firenze . . . ," *Bolletino d'arte,* IV (1910), pp. 297ff.

284. J. LUTZ and P. Perdrizet, *Speculum humanae Salvationis,* Leipzig, 1907ff.

294. (ANTONIO MANETTI), *Vita di Filippo Brunelleschi,* ed. E. Toesca, Rome, 1927.

301. R. VAN MARLE, *The Development of the Italian Schools of Painting,* The Hague, 1923ff.

306. H. M. R. MARTIN, *La miniature française du XIIIe au XVe siècle,* Paris, 1923.

372. H. A. OMONT, *Miniatures des plus anciens manuscrits grecs de la Bibliothèque Nationale du VIe au XIVe siècle,* Paris, 1929.

373. H. A. OMONT, *Les Miniatures du Psautier de Saint Louis,* Leyden, 1902.

427. U. PROCACCI, "Niccolo di Piero Lamberti . . . e Niccolo di Luca Spinelli," *Il Vasari,* I (1927–28), pp. 300ff.

492. F. R. SHAPLEY and C. K. KENNEDY, "Brunelleschi in Competition with Ghiberti," *Art Bulletin,* V (1922–23), pp. 31ff.

507. L. STORNAIOLO, *Le miniature della Topografia Cristiana di Cosma Indicopleuste,* Milan, 1918.

531. GIORGIO VASARI, *Le Vite de' piu eccellenti architetti, pittori et scultori Italiani,* Florence, 1550, reprint, ed. C. Ricci, Milan and Rome, 1927.

533. GIORGIO VASARI, *Le vite de' piu eccellenti pittori, scultori ed architettori (Le opere di G. Vasari:* I–VIII, *Le Vite;* VIII, *I ragionamenti e lettere),* Florence, 1878ff; quoted as *Vasari-Milanesi.*

Giovanni Cavalcanti
Criticism of Brunelleschi, in
History of Florence (ca. 1440)

[In Florence] there were some capricious people (among whom was Filippo di ser Brunellesco) who advised, and with their false and deceitful science of geometry (not in itself, but in the ignorance of others) demonstrated, that the city of Lucca could be flooded, and therefore with their arts which were not well learned they devised a scheme and the foolish people cheered that it had been done.[1]

The Italian text is found in G. Cavalcanti, *Istorie Fiorentine,* Book VI, Chapter XVIII, ed. F. Polidori (Florence, 1838), I, 328.

---

[1] [Of interest is Polidori's footnote to this passage: "It is sad to see named with so little respect a man of such genius and so deserving of the glory of his country. It is, however, necessary to realize that this idea [to flood Lucca] would have brought little honor to Brunelleschi under any circumstances. Vasari (in his biography of Brunelleschi) did not even mention it, and Neri Capponi (an important fifteenth-century Florentine, active in the political life of the city, and one of its chroniclers—Ed.), who actually saw Brunelleschi's plan and *laughed at it* and for two entire days tried to keep it from being accepted, was well aware of the weakness of the enterprise when he said 'the gentlemen of Lucca will demolish the embankment and the water will return to the Serchio River.' . . ."—Ed.]

Niccolò Machiavelli (1469–1527)

Criticism of Brunelleschi, in
History of Florence (ca. 1520)

At that time [1430] there lived in Florence a distinguished architect named Filippo di Ser Brunellesco, of whose works our city is full; such were his merits that after his death his statue in marble was put in the main church in Florence with an inscription beneath it that to all who read it still bears testimony to his ability. He demonstrated that Lucca could be flooded because of the position of the city in relation to the bend of the river Serchio, and he argued so well that the Ten[1] arranged to have his plan tried. From it came nothing more than trouble for our army and security for the enemy; for the Lucchese raised the level of the land with a levee built in the place where our army was [newly] directing the Serchio River; then one night they demolished the embankment of the canal by which our army was conducting the waters [of the river] so that the water, finding a high barrier in the direction of Lucca but the embankment of the canal open, flooded the entire plain; hence [our] army instead of being able to come near the city had to retreat.

The Italian text is found in N. Machiavelli, *Istorie Fiorentine*, Book IV, Chapter XXIII, in *Opere*, ed. M. Bonfantini (Milan-Naples, 1963), 755.

[1] [The Council on War.—Ed.]

Antonio di Tuccio Manetti

From *The*

Life of Brunelleschi (1480's)

Girolamo, you wish to know who that Filippo was who played the practical joke you admire so much on il Grasso, the true account of which I related to you. Having been, according to the epitaph, a Florentine of the not too distant past, you want to know of what family he came; whether he—or his family—has descendants; why he was granted the great distinction of being buried in Santa Maria del Fiore and why the marble bust, which they say was carved from life, was placed there in perpetual memory with such a splendid epitaph; and in what year of grace he was born and in what year he died. I will gladly give you all the information I have about him, which is not a great deal, first of all regarding this question of yours and also so that you may read the narrative as a true account and not as a fable like many that are written; and because you will, given your intelligence and this opportunity, comprehend it all—something much easier for you than for many others; and because in this way I shall be able to satisfy you more than I have sometimes done in words when you asked how that manner of building, called *alla Romana* or *alla antica,* that is attempted so vainly today, was restored, and by whom it was brought back to light, since earlier buildings were all German and called modern. You will learn that he was a man of great intellect, great resoluteness, and extraordinary talent. In certain parts you will see

From *The Life of Brunelleschi* by Antonio di Tuccio Manetti, pp. 34, 38, 40, 42, 44, 46, 50, 52, 54, 66, 68, 94. Introduction, Notes, and Critical Text Edition by Howard Saalman. English translation by Catherine Enggass. Published by the Pennsylvania State University Press, University Park and London. Copyright © 1970 by The Pennsylvania State University. Reprinted by permission.

how far and to what extent credit may be given to him and what was deserving of honor. You will see of which of the building methods used in public and private edifices today he might almost be said to have been the inventor. If some defects are noted in the buildings that he began and of which he was the inventor, they are not due to him, but to others. You will discover—unless the facts are unknown—to whom these defects were due.

Since you have read the epitaph I will concentrate more on those facts not recorded there. You will understand what I mean to say in spite of the words which, although factual, might have been put together by an idiot; and do not be annoyed because I do not follow the order outlined above.

Filippo di Ser Brunellesco, architect, was of our city and in my time I knew him and spoke to him. He came of good and honorable people. He was born in the year of Our Lord 1377 in our city and there, for the most part, he lived, and there, according to the flesh, he died. . . .

Following the general custom of men of standing in Florence, Filippo learned to read and write at an early age and to use the abacus. He also learned some Latin; perhaps because his father, who was a notary, thought of having him follow the same profession, since very few men in that period took up Latin—or were made to take it up—unless they expected to become a doctor, notary, or priest. He was very obedient, manageable, and fearful of disgrace. That fear was more effective than threats or any other device. He longed for distinction in whatever he undertook. From childhood he had a natural interest in drawing and painting and his work was very charming. For that reason he elected to become a goldsmith when his father, as was the custom, apprenticed him to a trade. Noting his aptitude, his father, who was a wise man, gave his consent.

Because of his foundation in drawing he quickly became very proficient in that profession in which he soon displayed himself most wonderfully. Within a brief period he became a complete master in niello, enamel, and ornamental architectural reliefs, as well as in cutting, mounting, and polishing all kinds of precious stones. It was in general the same in everything he dedicated himself to. In that art and what pertained to it he succeeded more marvelously than seemed possible at his age. That is the reason why he was commissioned in his youth to make certain large silver figures to be added to the very rich altar in San Jacopo in Pistoia. They were made by him, as he was a master although very young. He carved and painted a very beautiful life-size—or little less than life-size—wooden statue in the round of St. Mary Magdalen which was destroyed when the church of Santo Spirito burned in 1471. He carved in wood and painted a life-size crucifix in the round. It is attached to the pillar between the two side chapels on the side of the transept toward the old piazza in Santa Maria Novella. In the opinion of connoisseurs it is unsurpassed for excellence in sculpture, especially that of crucifixes. According to reports of his contemporaries he created other very beautiful works in bronze and other materials. However, all those I have mentioned I have seen.

Since, as we said, he revealed a marvelous genius, his advice about buildings was in great demand. His kinsman Apollonio Lapi employed him a great deal when he was building the house by the Canto de'Ricci toward the Mercato Vecchio, which now belongs to his son Bartolomeo. There is much that is good, comfortable, and pleasing to be seen on the inside; however, during that period the method of building was very crude as may be observed in contemporary and earlier buildings.

It is reported that when the construction of Villa Petraia was undertaken Filippo's advice was requested by the proprietor of the holding and that the tower was built in accordance with his advice. Although people have praised the tower to me, I have only seen it from a distance. The construction was interrupted because of a change of fortune [in the family].

When he was a young man it was necessary to construct the office and residence for the officials of the Monte as well as the room for their assistants in that part of the Signoria where there used to be mainly columned loggias. The loggias had been built for the beauty and splendor of the palace; they were much admired in their time and are still to be seen there. Filippo was asked to act as architect, designer, and director of construction in this undertaking and he did so. That he did not like the architectural details used in those days and did not use them can still be noted. He did it in a different way, but the manner which he later acquired after he had seen the ancient buildings of the Romans was not yet his.

During the same period he propounded and realized what painters today call perspective, since it forms part of that science which, in effect, consists of setting down properly and rationally the reductions and enlargements of near and distant objects as perceived by the eye of man: buildings, plains, mountains, places of every sort and location, with figures and objects in correct proportion to the distance in which they are shown. He originated the rule that is essential to whatever has been accomplished since his time in that area. We do not know whether centuries ago the ancient painters—who in that period of fine sculptors are believed to have been good masters—knew about perspective or employed it rationally. If indeed they employed it by rule (I did not previously call it a science without reason) as he did later, whoever could have imparted it to him had been dead for centuries and no written records about it have been discovered, or if they have been, have not been comprehended. Through industry and intelligence he either rediscovered or invented it.

Although he was preëminent over many others in many things and consequently refined his own and the following century, he was never known to boast or praise himself or vaunt or laud himself by a single word. Instead he proved himself by his deeds with the opportunities that came along. Unless greatly provoked by insulting or disrespectful acts, he never became angry and was amiable to his friends. It gave him pleasure to commend those who merited it. He willingly instructed those he thought wished to be instructed and who were capable of instruction. He was very skillful and discerning in that as he was in other things.

He first demonstrated his system of perspective on a small panel about half a *braccio* square. He made a representation of the exterior of San Giovanni in Florence, encompassing as much of that temple as can be seen at a glance from the outside. In order to paint it it seems that he stationed himself some three *braccia* inside the central portal of Santa Maria del Fiore. He painted it with such care and delicacy and with such great precision in the black and white colors of the marble that no miniaturist could have done it better. In the foreground he painted that part of the piazza encompassed by the eye, that is to say, from the side facing the Misericordia up to the arch and corner of the sheep [market], and from the side with the column of the miracle of St. Zenobius up to the corner of the straw [market], and all that is seen in that area for some distance. And he placed burnished silver where the sky had to be represented, that is to say, where the buildings of the painting were free in the air, so that the real air and atmosphere were reflected in it, and thus the clouds seen in the silver are carried along by the wind as it blows. Since in such a painting it is necessary that the painter postulate beforehand a single point from which his painting must be viewed, taking into account the length and width of the sides as well as the distance, in order that no error would be made in looking at it (since any point outside of that single point would change the shapes to the eye), he made a hole in the painted panel at that point in the temple of San Giovanni which is directly opposite the eye of anyone stationed inside the central portal of Santa Maria del Fiore, for the purpose of painting it. The hole was as tiny as a lentil bean on the painted side and it widened conically like a woman's straw hat to about the circumference of a ducat, or a bit more, on the reverse side. He required that whoever wanted to look at it place his eye on the reverse side where the hole was large, and while bringing the hole up to his eye with one hand, to hold a flat mirror with the other hand in such a way that the painting would be reflected in it. The mirror was extended by the other hand a distance that more or less approximated in small *braccia* the distance in regular *braccia* from the place he appears to have been when he painted it up to the church of San Giovanni. With the aforementioned elements of the burnished silver, the piazza, the viewpoint, etc., the spectator felt he saw the actual scene when he looked at the painting. I have had it in my hands and seen it many times in my days and can testify to it.

He made a perspective of the piazza of the Palazzo dei Signori in Florence together with all that is in front of it and around it that is encompassed by the eye when one stands outside the piazza, or better, along the front of the church of San Romolo beyond the Canto di Calimala Francesca, which opens into that piazza a few feet toward Orto San Michele. From that position two entire façades—the west and the north—of the Palazzo dei Signori can be seen. It is marvelous to see, with all the objects the eye absorbs in that place, what appears. Paolo Uccello and other painters came along later and wanted to copy and imitate it. I have seen more than one of these efforts and none was done as well as his.

One might ask at this point why, since it was a perspective, he did not make that aperture for the eye in this painting as he did in the small panel of the Duomo of San Giovanni? The reason that he did not was because the panel for such a large piazza had to be large enough to set down all those many diverse objects, thus it could not be held up with one hand while holding a mirror in the other hand like the San Giovanni panel: no matter how far it is extended a man's arm is not sufficiently long or sufficiently strong to hold the mirror opposite the point with its distance. He left it up to the spectator's judgment, as is done in paintings by other artists, even though at times this is not discerning. And where in the San Giovanni panel he had placed burnished silver, here he cut away the panel in the area above the buildings represented, and took it to a spot in which he could observe it with the natural atmosphere above the buildings. . . .

[Manetti's account of the contest for the Baptistery Door appears at this point in his text. See above, pp. 38ff.—Ed.]

Thus left out, Filippo seemed to say: my knowledge was not sufficient for them to entrust me with the whole undertaking; it would be a good thing to go where there is fine sculpture to observe. So he went to Rome where at that time one could see beautiful works in public places. Some of those works are still there, although not many; some have been removed, carried off, and shipped out by various popes and cardinals from Rome and other nations. In studying the sculpture as one with a good eye, intelligent and alert in all things, would do, he observed the method and the symmetry of the ancients' way of building. He seemed to recognize very clearly a certain arrangement of members and structure just as if God had enlightened him about great matters. Since this appeared very different from the method in use at that time, it impressed him greatly. And he decided that while he looked at the sculpture of the ancients to give no less time to that order and method which is in the abutments and thrusts of buildings, [their] masses, lines, and *invenzioni* according to and in relation with their function, and to do the same for the decorations. Thereby he observed many marvels and beautiful things, since for the most part they were built in diverse epochs by very fine masters, who became so through practical experience and through the opportunity to study afforded by the large compensation of the princes and because they were not ordinary men. He decided to rediscover the fine and highly skilled method of building and the harmonious proportions of the ancients and how they might, without defects, be employed with convenience and economy. Noting the great and complex elements making up these matters—which had nevertheless been resolved—did not make him change his mind about understanding the methods and means they used. And by virtue of having in the past been interested and having made clocks and alarm bells with various and sundry types of springs geared by many diverse contrivances, he was familiar with all or a great number of those contrivances, which helped him a great deal in conceiving different machines for carrying, lifting, and pulling, according to what the exigencies were. He committed some of them to memory and some not, according to how important he judged them to be. He saw ruins—both standing or fallen down for some reason or other —which had been vaulted in various ways. He considered the methods of centering the vaults and other systems of support, how they could be dispensed with and what method had to be used, and when—because of the size of the vault or for other reasons—armatures could not be used. He saw and reflected on the many beautiful things, which as far as is known had not been present in other masters from antique times. By his genius, through tests and experiments, with time and with great effort and careful thought, he became a complete master of these matters in secret, while pretending to be doing something else. He demonstrated that mastery later in our city and elsewhere, as this account will in part make known.

The sculptor Donatello was with him almost all the time during this stay in Rome. They originally went there in agreement about strictly sculptural matters, and they applied themselves constantly to these. Donatello had no interest in architecture. Filippo told him nothing of his ideas, either because he did not find Donatello apt or because he was not confident of prevailing, seeing more every minute the difficulties confronting him. However, together they made rough drawings of almost all the buildings in Rome and in many places beyond the walls, with measurements of the widths and heights as far as they were able to ascertain [the latter] by estimation, and also the lengths, etc. In many places they had excavations made in order to see the junctures of the membering of the buildings and their type—whether square, polygonal, completely round, oval, or whatever. When possible they estimated the heights [by measuring] from base to base for the height and similarly [they estimated the heights of] the entablatures and roofs from the foundations. They drew the elevations on strips of parchment graphs with numbers and symbols which Filippo alone understood.

Since both were good masters of the goldsmith's art, they earned their living in that craft. They were given more work to do in the goldsmiths' shops every day than they could handle. And Filippo cut many precious stones given him to dress. Neither of them had family problems since they had neither wife nor children, there or elsewhere. Neither of them paid much attention to what they ate and drank or how they were dressed or where they lived, as long as they were able to satisfy themselves by seeing and measuring.

Since they undertook excavations to find the junctures of the membering and to uncover objects and buildings in many places where there was some indication, they had to hire porters and other laborers at no small expense. No one else attempted such work or understood why they did it. This lack of understanding was due to the fact that during that period, and for hundreds of years before, no one paid attention to the classical method of building: if certain writers in pagan times gave precepts about that method, such as Battista degli Alberti has done in our period, they were not much more than generalities. However, the *invenzioni*—those things peculiar to the master—were in large part the product of empirical investigation or of his own [theoretical] efforts.

Returning to the excavations of Filippo and Donato: they were generally called "the treasure hunters" as it was believed that they spent and looked for treasure. They said: The treasure hunters search here today and there tomorrow. Actually they sometimes, although rarely, found some silver or gold medals, carved stones, chalcedony, carnelians, cameos, and like objects. From that in large measure arose the belief that they were searching for treasure.

Filippo spent many years at this work. He found a number of differences among the beautiful and rich elements of the buildings— in the masonry, as well as in the types of columns, bases, capitals, architraves, friezes, cornices, and pediments, and differences between the masses of the temples and the diameters of the columns; by means of close observation he clearly recognized the characteristics of each type: Ionic, Doric, Tuscan, Corinthian, and Attic. As may still be seen in his buildings today, he used most of them at the time and place he considered best. . . .

After all these very important considerations and preparations, as well as many others which will be left out in order not to become tedious, they came to the problem of how to vault it [Florence Cathedral], that great, heavy, double vault, which is of such great weight throughout. That the vault had to be supported with centering was taken for granted by all the masters except Filippo. And since each master expressed his own opinion of what method to use, two conclusions were drawn from Filippo's speech. The first being that such a great undertaking could not be accomplished with centering: the second being that they were obliged, if they wished to vault it, to do so without centering. Not having proved himself in any large undertaking comparable to this building, and this building having to be such as it later appeared and as was then anticipated—and not having sufficient influence at that time to satisfy everyone, he was ridiculed by the *operai* and other ordinary citizens and no less by our own masters than by the foreign masters, of whom there were a good number chosen from all parts. From Filippo's words the *operai* unanimously drew the conclusion that a large building of such a character could not be completed and that it had been naïve of earlier masters and those who relied on them to believe [that it could be finished]. When Filippo protested against this erroneous conclusion which he saw they had accepted, and when he told them it could be done, they united in one in asking: How will it be supported? He repeated constantly that it could be vaulted without centering. After many days of standing firm—he in his opinion and they in theirs—he was twice angrily carried out by the servants of the *operai* and of the Wool Merchants Guild, the consuls, and many others present, as if he were reasoning foolishly and his words were laughable. As a consequence he was later often wont to say that during the period in which that occurred (some days elapsed between the first and second occasion) he was ashamed to go about Florence. He had the feeling that behind his back they were saying: Look at that mad man who utters such nonsense. However, he persevered in his judgment with great prudence, caution, and incredible patience, constantly praising others when he could do so in fairness and rendering honor to those who merited it, holding the esteem of the *operai* and the other citizens—except in this case—for the valiant, prudent, ingenious man that he was.

Seeing his persistence, some people began to heed him, especially because of the difficulty and almost impossibility demonstrated generally, in one way or another, by all the others. . . .

Thus, on returning home some heed began to be paid to him in certain quarters. They began to accept the reasons he had outlined and to ask whether he might not be trusted in the great undertaking if he could provide some confirmation in a small undertaking, stating that since Schiatta Ridolfi had to have a chapel constructed in San Jacopo di Borgo Oltrarno and since Filippo knew about it he could show them what he could do in that chapel. And so he did. It was the first in Florence to be vaulted in that form which is still called "with crests and sails." . . .

By these means and many others he proceeded in such a way that the completion of the cupolas arrived with great beauty, with strength, with provisions for any eventuality, with savings for the *opera*, without defect, with the great satisfaction of everyone—whether knowledgeable or ignorant—who saw it, and with the greatest fame and glory for himself. Everyone believed that only one person in the world could have accomplished it and that was the one who had done it, by which was meant that it was truly the work of God.

During his life not a small stone or brick was placed which he did not wish to examine to see whether it was correct and if it was well-fired and cleaned: something which no care was expended upon afterward, since today attention is paid only to what appears to be economical, and stones from the river and rough bricks and all sorts of crudity are employed. The care he gave to the mortar was wonderful. He personally went to the brickyards regarding the stones and the baking, the sand and lime mixture, and whatever was required. He seemed to be the master of everything.

For that reason they sent for him for whatever had to be built of importance in or out of the city: public or private, sacred or secular, fortresses, or any sort of building, or machinery, or any similar undertaking. Many lords wrote to the Signoria and to the leaders to obtain the favor of engaging him and he had to go to many places. Anything he advised and proposed appeared to the greatest admiration and to a flood of all sorts of praise. This occurred to no lesser degree in our city.

For that reason he was proposed for many public and private buildings. According to what was required he had to make plans and models for them. When he was away in this or that community or with this or that Prince, some of the buildings were spoiled by failing in one way or another to carry out his orders exactly, either because of ignorance or presumption. . . .

Giorgio Vasari (1511–1574)
From the Biography of
Brunelleschi, in *Lives of the*
Painters, Sculptors, and Architects
(1550)

It frequently happens that men of insignificant appearance possess great generosity of spirit and sincerity of heart, and when nobility of soul is joined to these characteristics the greatest marvels may be expected, for they endeavour to overcome the defects of their body by the virtues of their mind. This appears in Filippo di ser Brunellesco, as well as in Messer Forese da Rabatta and Giotto, who were all of mean appearance, but their minds were lofty, and of Filippo it may be said that he was given by Heaven to invest architecture with new forms, after it had wandered astray for many centuries, during which the men of the time had expended much treasure to bad purpose in erecting buildings devoid of arrangement, in bad style, of sorry design, with the queerest notions, most ungraceful grace, and worse ornament. It was Heaven's decree, after the earth had been so many years without a master mind and divine spirit, that Filippo should leave to the world the greatest and loftiest building, the finest of all the achievements of

From the book *Lives of the Painters, Sculptors and Architects* by Giorgio Vasari. Ed. by Wm. Gaunt. Trans. by A. B. Hinds. Everyman's Library Edition. Published by E. P. Dutton & Co., Inc., New York, and J. M. Dent & Sons, Ltd., London, and used with their permission. Vol. I, portions from pp. 269–78, 281–82, 287–88, 290–91, 293–95, 297–300, with footnotes.

ancient and modern times, proving that the ability of the Tuscan artists though lost was not dead. It also adorned him with the highest virtues, among which was that of friendship, and no one was ever more kind and loveable than he. His judgment was free from passion, and when he perceived merit in others he put aside his own interest and that of his friends. He knew himself and communicated his own virtues to many, being always ready to assist his neighbours when in need. The mortal enemy of vice, he sought the society of those who practised virtue. He never wasted time, but was always engaged upon his own works or those of others, if they needed help, and was always visiting his friends and remembering them. . . .

In [Brunelleschi's] early youth his father carefully taught him the first principles of letters, in which he exhibited much intelligence, but he did not exert his full powers, as if he did not wish to attain to great perfection in this, intending apparently to devote himself to things of greater utility. This greatly displeased Ser Brunellesco, who wished to make him a notary or to follow his great-great-grandfather's profession. But perceiving that the boy was always returning to art and manual work, he made him learn the abacus and writing and then put him with a goldsmith, a friend of his, so that he should learn to design. Greatly delighted, Filippo began to learn and practise that art, so that before many years he could set stones better than a practised craftsman. He did niello and grotesques, such as half-length silver figures of two prophets placed at the head of the altar of S. Jacopo of Pistoia[1] and considered very beautiful, made by him for the wardens of the city, and works in bas-relief where he showed such a thorough grasp of that trade that his mind was clearly ready to pass to higher things. Coming into contact with some studious artists he began to study with enthusiasm motion, weights and wheels, how they may be made to revolve and what sets them in motion, and so produced with his own hand some excellent and very beautiful clocks. Not contented with this he aspired to practise sculpture on a large scale, and this led to a constant association in practising that art with Donatello, a youth of skill and great promise, and so great an affection grew up between them, owing to their high qualities, that they did not seem able to live apart from one another. Although Filippo was skilled in many things and prac-

---

[1] In 1400.

tised several professions, yet he did not devote so much time to them as to prevent his being considered an excellent architect by persons qualified to judge. He proved this in his decorations for various houses, such as that of Appollonio Lapi, his kinsman, at the corner of the Ciai towards the Mercato Vecchio, where he did many things during the building. Outside Florence he did the same in the tower and house of the Petraia at Castello. In the palace of the Signoria he arranged and separated off all the apartments where the offices of the officials of the Monte were situated, and constructed the doors and windows in a style borrowed from the ancients not much in use then, because architecture was in a very crude state in Tuscany. Filippo was next commissioned to make a statue in linden wood of St. Mary Magdalene in penitence for the friars of S. Spirito, to be placed in a chapel, and as he had made many small things in sculpture he was anxious to prove that he could also succeed in large ones. When the statue was finished and set up it was considered most beautiful, but it perished in the fire at that church in 1471, together with many other notable things. He paid great attention to perspective, which was badly understood at the time, many errors being perpetrated, and spent much time over it, but at length he discovered unaided a method of getting it perfectly true; this was to trace it with the ground plan and elevation by means of intersecting lines, a useful addition to the art of design. He took such delight in this that he drew with his own hand the piazza of S. Giovanni, with all the divisions of the black and white marble incrustation, diminishing them with a singular grace; and he also did the house of the Misericordia, with the shops of the wafer-makers; the vault of the Pecori, with the column of St. Zanobi on the other side. The praise accorded to the work by artists and connoisseurs so much encouraged him that before long he began another, drawing the palace, the piazza and the loggia of the Signori, with the shelter of the Pisani and all the buildings about, thus awakening the spirit of other artists, who afterwards bestowed much study upon them. In particular, he taught Masaccio the painter, then a youth and his close friend, who did honour to his ininstructor, as appears in the buildings which occur in his works. He further showed it to those who do tarsia work, which is an art of inlaying coloured woods, stimulating them to such an extent that he gave rise to many good and useful things produced in that art both then and afterwards which have brought fame and profit to Florence for many years. One evening Messer Paolo dal Pozzo Toscanelli happened to be entertaining some friends in a garden and invited Filippo, who, hearing him speak of mathematics, cultivated his friendship and learned geometry from him, and, although Filippo was not a lettered man, he was able to argue so well from his own practice and experience that he often astonished M. Paolo. Then again Filippo interested himself in the Christian Scriptures, and never failed to be present at the disputes and preaching of learned persons, making so much profit through his excellent memory that M. Paolo used to say that when he heard Filippo argue he thought he was listening to a new St. Paul. At this time also Filippo studied Dante, thoroughly familiarising himself with the localities and measurements, and often quoting the poet in his arguments. His mind was always contriving and imagining ingenious and difficult things, and he found a kindred spirit in Donato, with whom he would have friendly discussions, in which they both delighted, on the difficulties of their profession. Thus, one day when Donato had finished a wooden crucifix (which was placed in S. Croce in Florence, under the scene where St. Francis raises the child, painted by Taddeo Gaddi), he wished to have Filippo's opinion; but he repented, for Filippo said that he had put a rustic on the cross. Donato then retorted, "Take some wood and make one yourself," as is related at length in his life. Filippo, who never lost his temper, however great the provocation, quietly worked on for several months until he had completed a wooden crucifix of the same size, of extraordinary excellence, and designed with great art and diligence. He then sent Donato to his house before him, quite ignorant of the fact that Filippo had made such a work, so that he broke an apron-full of eggs and things for their meal which he had with him, while he regarded the marvel with transport, noting the art and skill shown by Filippo in the legs, body and arms of the figure, the whole being so finely and harmoniously composed that Donato not only acknowledged himself beaten but proclaimed the work as a miracle. It is now placed in S. Maria Novella, between the Chapel of the Strozzi and that of the Bardi of Vernio, where it is still greatly admired by the moderns. . . . [Vasari's account of the contest for the Baptistery Door appears at this point in his text. See above, pp. 42ff.—Ed.]

After the doors had been allotted to Lorenzo Ghiberti, Filippo and Donato met, and determined to leave Florence and go to Rome for a year or so, the one to study architecture and the other sculpture.

Filippo did this because he wished to be superior to Lorenzo and Donato, since architecture is much more useful to men than either painting or sculpture. After Filippo had sold a small property of his at Settignano, they left Florence and proceeded to Rome, where at the sight of the grandeur of the buildings, and the perfection of the churches, Filippo was lost in wonder, so that he looked like one demented. He set to work to measure the cornices and take the plans of these buildings. He and Donato were constantly going about and spared neither time nor money. They left no place unvisited, either in Rome or its neighbourhood, and took measurements of everything when they had the opportunity. As Filippo was free from the cares of a family, he abandoned himself to his studies, neglecting to sleep and to eat, his only concern being architecture, which had been corrupted, studying the good ancient orders and not the barbarous Gothic style then in general use. Two great ideals possessed him: the one to bring back to light the true architecture, whereby he believed he should make a name for himself not inferior to that of Giotto and Cimabue, the other was to find a method, if possible, of vaulting the cupola of S. Maria del Fiore at Florence, the difficulty of which had deterred anyone, after the death of Arnolfo Lapi, from wishing to attempt it, except by incurring a great expense for a wooden covering. However, he did not communicate this purpose of his to Donato or to any living soul, but in Rome he attentively observed all the difficulties of the vaulting of the Rotonda. He had noted and drawn all the vaulting in the antique, and he was continually studying the subject, and if pieces of capitals, columns, cornices and bases of buildings were found buried he and Donato set to work and dug them out to find the foundations. From this a report spread in Rome, when they passed by, carelessly dressed, and they were called the men of the treasure, for it was believed that they were studying necromancy in order to find treasure. The reason for this was that one day they had found an ancient earthen vessel full of medals. Filippo came to be short of money and he went about setting precious jewels for some goldsmiths, friends of his. On Donato returning to Florence he was left alone, and he studied the more ardently and diligently among the ruins of ancient buildings. He drew every sort of building, round and square, and octagonal churches, basilicas, aqueducts, baths, arches, coliseums, amphitheatres, and every temple of brick, noting the methods of binding and clamping as well as the turning of the vaulting. Finding by examination that all the large stones had a hole in the middle of the under-side, for the iron tool used for drawing the stones up, called by us the *ulivella,* he reintroduced this system and brought it into general use. He then studied the Doric, Ionic and Corinthian orders, one after the other, and to such purpose that he was able to reconstruct in his mind's eye the aspect of Rome as it stood before its fall.

The air of the city caused him a slight disorder in the year 1407, and he was advised by his friends to take a change. Accordingly he returned to Florence, where many buildings had suffered by his absence, and on his arrival he was enabled to supply many designs and much advice. The same year there took place a gathering of architects and engineers of the district upon the method of vaulting the cupola, at the instance of the wardens of S. Maria del Fiore and the consuls of the art of wool. In this Filippo took part.

He remained many months at Florence, where he secretly made many models and machines, all designed for the work of the cupola, always joking with his fellow-artists.

On his arrival [after his sojourn in Rome], the wardens of S. Maria del Fiore and the consuls of the art of wool met together and told him all the difficulties, from the least to the greatest, which had been raised by the masters, who were also present. Filippo answered as follows: "Wardens, there is no doubt that great things always present difficulties in their execution, and this particular one offers questions especially hard to solve, harder than you are perhaps aware. I do not know if even the ancients ever vaulted anything so tremendous as this, and I have often thought of the framework, both within and without, and how it might be safely constructed, and I have never been able to make up my mind, for the breadth of the building troubles me no less than its height. If it had been circular, it would have been possible to follow the methods observed by the Romans in vaulting the Pantheon or Rotonda at Rome, but here it is necessary to follow the eight sides, and to dovetail and chain the stones together, questions of great difficulty. But when I remember that the church is dedicated to God and to the Virgin, I am confident that what is done in their memory will not fail for lack of knowledge, and that the architect will receive aid in his strength, wisdom and ingenuity. But of what assistance can I be, as the work is none of mine? However, I will say that if the work were entrusted to me, I should resolutely set myself to find a means of vaulting it without too much trouble; but I have not yet thought of the matter, and yet you wish me to find a means! But if you propose to have it vaulted, you should not appeal to me only, for I do not think I am competent to give advice on so great a matter, but you should ordain that within a year, and on an appointed day, architects shall come to Florence, not only Tuscans and Italians, but Germans, French, and others, to give their advice, so that, after the question has been discussed and settled by so many masters, the work may be begun, and be entrusted to the man who will give proof of the best methods and ability to carry it out. I can give you no better advice than this." This suggestion of Filippo pleased the consuls and wardens, but they would have preferred him to have made a model in the meantime, and to have devoted his attention to the question. But he affected carelessness, and, having taken leave of them, said that he had received letters requesting him to return to Rome. When the consuls perceived that their prayers, united with those of the wardens, could not detain him, they induced many of his friends to use their influence, and as this did not succeed, one morning, on the 26th May, 1417, the wardens decreed him an allowance of money, which is to be found debited to him in the books of the opera, all this being done to satisfy him. But he remained firm to his purpose, and leaving Florence he returned to Rome, where he devoted himself to constant study in preparation for this great work, for he felt confident that no one but himself could carry it out. . . .

When Filippo had finished writing [his plan], he went in the morning to the magistrates and, on his showing them this sheet, they proceeded to consider it, and although they were not able to grasp it, yet, seeing the confidence of Filippo and that none of the other architects were on more certain ground, while he always exhibited the utmost assurance in his replies, which would have led one to suppose that he had already vaulted ten such spaces, the consuls withdrew apart and proposed to give him the work. However, they wished to be shown how the vaulting could be made without a framework, though they approved of all the rest. Fortune favoured this desire, for since Bartolommeo Barbadori had previously proposed to erect a chapel at S. Felicita, and had consulted Filippo about it, the latter had undertaken the work, and caused the chapel to be vaulted without a framework. It is on the right as one enters the church, as is the holy-water vessel by the same hand. About the same time Filippo vaulted another chapel at S. Jacopo sopr' Arno for Stiatta Ridolfi, next to the chapel of the high altar, and these things inspired more confidence than his arguments. The consuls and the wardens being thus reassured by the document and the work which they had seen, allotted the cupola to him, making him head master by a majority of votes. . . .

The murmurers [Brunelleschi's critics] had now been silenced, and the genius of Filippo had so far triumphed in the smooth progress of the building, that all who were not blinded by passion considered that he had displayed more ability in this structure than almost any other artist, ancient or modern. This feeling was caused by his producing his model, by which he showed with what care he had considered every detail: the ladders, the lights within and without, so that no one could injure himself in the darkness, and various iron staples for the purpose of mounting where it was steep, and similar considerations. Besides this, he had devised the iron staples to bear the scaffolding inside if it was ever to be adorned with mosaics or painting, and had put in the least dangerous places the channels for carrying off the water, showing where they should be covered, and where uncovered, arranging spaces and apertures to break the force of the winds, and to provide that tempests and earthquakes should not injure the structure, in all which things he proved how much he had profited by the long years he spent at Rome. When one considers how much attention he had paid to the joints, incrustations, nailing and ties of stone, one trembles at the thought that a single mind could compass so much. So greatly did his abilities increase that there was nothing, however difficult and hard, which he did not render easy and smooth. . . .

With his own hand he made the model of the chapter-house of S. Croce in Florence for the family of the Pazzi,[2] a work of great and varied beauty, and the model of the house of the Busini[3] for the use of two families, and also the model for the house and loggia of the Innocenti,[4] the vaulting of which was erected without a scaffolding, a method now universally adopted. It is said that Filippo was invited to Milan to make the model for a fortress for the duke, Filippo Maria,

[2] Begun 1429.
[3] Now Quaratesi, via Proconsolo, begun 1445. [Vasari is referring to Palazzo Quaratesi in Piazza d'Ognissanti.—Ed.]
[4] Begun 1420.

and that he left the care of the structure of the Innocenti to his close friend, Francesco della Luna. This Francesco made the surrounding ornamentation of an architrave, running downward from above, which is false according to architecture. When Filippo returned and blamed him for this, he replied that he had taken it from the church of S. Giovanni, which is ancient. "It is the only error in that building," replied Filippo, "and you have copied it." The model of this building by Filippo's hand was for many years in the art of Por S. Maria, and much valued as the structure was to have been completed. To-day it is lost. Filippo made the model of the abbey of the Regular Canons of Fiesole for Cosimo de' Medici. It is a very ornate architecture, convenient and delightful; in fine really magnificent. The church with its barrel vaulting is roomy, the sacristy has its own conveniences, and indeed so has every other part of the monastery. . . .

Filippo also designed the model of the fortress of Vicopisano, and at Pisa he designed the old citadel and fortified the sea bridge, while he further designed the new citadel for enclosing the bridge with the two towers. He also made the model of the fortress of the harbour of Pesaro, and on his return to Milan he did many things for the duke, including plans for the builders of the Duomo. At that time the church of S. Lorenzo at Florence was begun[5] by order of the parishioners, . . . Giovanni [di Bicci de' Medici] and the others had proposed to make the choir in the middle under the tribune. At Filippo's desire Cosimo moved it, so as to increase the size of the large chapel, which had been a small recess in the first design, and to be able to place the choir there as it now is. When this was finished, the middle tribune and the rest of the church still remained to be done, and these were not vaulted until after Filippo's death. The church is 144 braccia long and it contains many errors, among others that the columns rest on the ground without a dado beneath, which ought to reach to the level of the bases of the pilasters, placed upon the steps. The pilaster thus looks shorter than the column, and gives the whole work a stunted appearance. This was due to the advice of those who survived Filippo, who envied his name, and who in his lifetime had made models against him. While Filippo lived he ridiculed them in his

[5] In 1419.

sonnets, but after his death they revenged themselves not only in this work, but in all that was left to them to do. Filippo left the model, and a part of the capitular buildings of the priests of S. Lorenzo was finished in which he made the cloister 144 braccia long.

Whilst this work was going on, Cosimo de' Medici wished to build his palace, and accordingly opened his mind to Filippo, who, putting aside every other care, made him a most beautiful large model for it. He wished to have it erected opposite S. Lorenzo, on the piazza, and standing alone. Filippo had given such free rein to his art that Cosimo thought the building too sumptuous and grand, and more to escape envy than expense, he refrained from putting the work in hand. While he was at work on the model, Filippo would say that he thanked Fortune for giving him such a chance, for he had a house to build, a thing he had desired for many years, and it had fallen to his lot to make one which he was anxious and able to do. But learning afterwards Cosimo's resolve not to put that work in hand, he wrathfully broke the design into a thousand pieces. After his palace had been erected upon another plan, Cosimo repented that he had not followed Filippo's, and used to say that he had never spoken to a man of greater intelligence and wit than Filippo. The latter also made the model for the curious temple of the Angeli for the noble family of the Scolari, which was left incomplete as it is to-day, because the Florentines in their difficulties had spent the money upon some necessities of the city, or as some say, in the war which supervened with the Lucchese . . . If this temple of the Angeli had been finished according to the model of Brunellesco, it would have been one of the finest in Italy, since the part that may now be seen cannot be too highly praised. The drawing by Filippo's hand for the ground plan and elevation of this octagonal church are in our book, with others of his designs. Filippo also planned a rich and magnificent palace for M. Luca Pitti outside the S. Niccolo gate at Florence in a place called Ruciano, but not at all like that which was begun by the same man in Florence, and carried as far as the second story, with such grandeur and magnificence that no finer piece of Tuscan work has yet been seen. . . .

It is said that the apparatus of the Paradise of S. Felice in the piazza of that city was invented by Filippo for the representation or feast of the Annunciation according to the time-honoured custom of the Florentines. This thing was truly marvellous, and displayed the ability and industry of the inventor. On high was a heaven full of living and moving figures, and a quantity of lights which flash in and out. . . .

After [a committee of citizens] had deliberated upon [the rebuilding of the Church of S. Spirito] Filippo was sent for and made a model comprising all the arrangements befitting a Christian church. He entirely reversed the plan of the church, as he was most anxious that the piazza should face the Arno, for it was there that all the people from Genoa, the Riviera, the Lunigiana, the Pisano and the Lucchese passed by, and they would see the magnificence of the structure. But as certain people were unwilling to allow their houses to be pulled down, Filippo's wish could not be carried out. Filippo then made the model of the church as well as of the friars' quarters in their present form.[6] The length of the church was 171 braccia, and its breadth 54 braccia, and it is so well arranged that no building could be richer, finer or more spacious in the disposition of its columns and other ornaments. Indeed, had it not been for the curse of those who, from lack of understanding more than anything else, spoil things beautifully begun, this would be the most perfect church in Christendom, as in some respects it is, being more beautiful and better divided than any other, although the model has not been followed, as is shown by some things begun outside which have not followed the dispositions of the interior for the doors and window decoration as shown in the model. It contains some errors attributed to Filippo which I pass over, for I do not believe that he would have fallen into them if he had continued the building of that church, all his work being done with great judgment, discretion, genius and art, and everything brought to perfection. This work puts the stamp of the highest worth upon his genius.

Filippo was witty in his conversation and acute in repartee, as for instance in the case of Lorenzo Ghiberti, who had bought a property at Monte Morello called Lepriano, on which he spent twice as much as he derived from it, and finally sold it in disgust. On being asked what was the best thing Lorenzo had done, Filippo replied, "The sale of Lepriano," possibly thinking that he owed him this because of their unfriendly relations. At last, having reached the great age of sixty-nine, Filippo passed to a better life on 16th April, 1446,

[6] The church was begun about 1436.

Fig. 1.

IL BUGGIANO:
Wall Monument with epitaph and portrait of
Brunelleschi. Florence Cathedral
(Photo: Luigi Artini).

Fig. 2.
Tombstone covering Brunelleschi's grave, discovered July 1972.
Florence Cathedral
(Photo: Fotochronache for La Nazione).

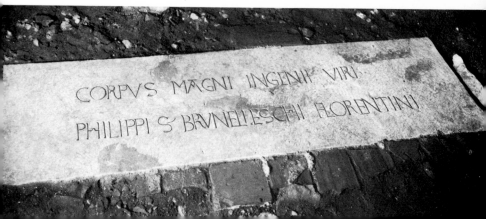

Fig. 3.
BRUNELLESCHI:
The Sacrifice of Isaac,
bronze relief. Florence,
Bargello *(Photo:
Alinari–Anderson)*.

Fig. 4.
GHIBERTI:
The Sacrifice of Isaac,
bronze relief.
Florence, Bargello
(Photo: Alinari–Anderson).

Fig. 5.
Florence Cathedral, Cupola,
from Piazza SS. Annunziata
(Photo: M. L. Trachtenberg).

Fig. 6.
Florence Cathedral, Cupola
(Photo: M. L. Trachtenberg)

Fig. 7.
Spedale degli Innocenti, loggia
(Photo: M. L. Trachtenberg).

Fig. 8.
Old Sacristy of San Lorenzo
(Photo: Alinari—Brogi).

Fig. 9.
San Lorenzo, nave columns
(Photo: M. L. Trachtenberg).

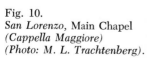

Fig. 10.
San Lorenzo, Main Chapel
(Cappella Maggiore)
(Photo: M. L. Trachtenberg).

Fig. 11.
Santo Spirito, side aisle
(Photo: Alinari).

Fig. 12.
Santo Spirito, side chapels
(Photo: Alinari).

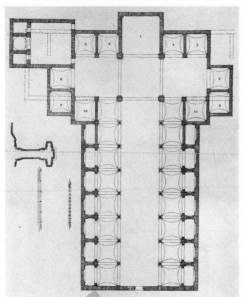

Fig. 13.
San Lorenzo, plan.

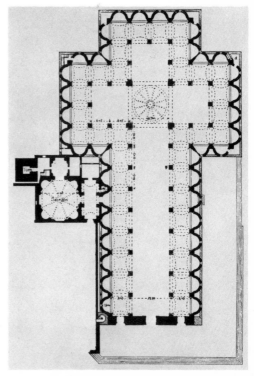

Fig. 14.
Santo Spirito, plan.

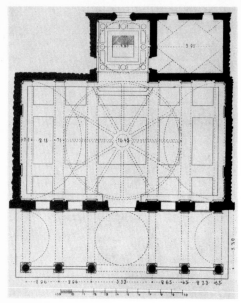

Fig. 15.
Pazzi Chapel, plan.

Fig. 16.
Santa Maria degli Angeli, plan.

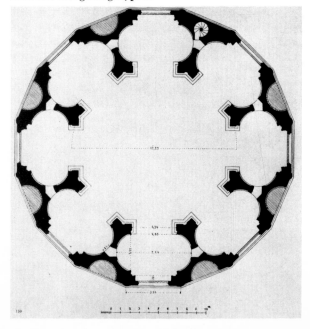

Fig. 17.
Pazzi Chapel, view
toward the apse
(Photo: Alinari—Anderson).

Fig. 18.
Pazzi Chapel, side wall
(Photo: Alinari—Brogi).

Fig. 19.
Santa Maria degli Angeli
(Photo: Alinari—Brogi).

Fig. 20.
Santa Maria degli Angeli, interior
(Photo: Alinari—Brogi).

Fig. 21.
Florence Cathedral, Lantern
(Photo: Alinari).

Fig. 22.
Florence Cathedral, detail of Lantern
(Photo: Alinari).

Fig. 23.
Florence Cathedral, Exedra
(Photo: M. L. Trachtenberg).

Fig. 24.
Florence Cathedral, detail of Exedra
(Photo: M. L. Trachtenberg).

after a life of labour in producing those works which should earn him an honoured name on earth and a place of rest in heaven. His loss caused great grief to his country, which knew him and valued him much more after his death than during his life. He was buried with honourable obsequies in S. Maria del Fiore. . . . It may safely be said that from the time of the ancient Greeks and Romans until now there has been no man more rare or more excellent than he, and he deserves the greater praise because in his time the Gothic style was admired in all Italy and practised by the old artists, as we see in a countless number of buildings. He reintroduced the ancient cornices and reinstated the Tuscan, Corinthian, Doric and Ionic orders in their original form. . . .

MODERN PERSPECTIVES
OF BRUNELLESCHI

Francesco Milizia (1725–1798)

From the Biographies of
Brunelleschi and Giacomo della
Porta, in *The Lives of Celebrated
Architects* (1768)

[Brunelleschi] finally applied himself to architecture, and learnt much from the Church of San Giovanni at Florence [the Baptistery] which is built in a good style, and very nearly approaching the antique; but of far greater importance to him was the attention he paid to the ancient monuments of Rome, the best of which he measured and sketched with great accuracy. To him is attributed the glory of having first revived the three ancient orders, the Doric, Ionic, and Corinthian. . . .

Brunelleschi conceived the idea of raising a cupola over the church of S. Maria del Fiore at Florence. . . . [He] completed his undertaking, which surpassed in height any work of the ancients. . . . The lantern alone remained imperfect; but he left a model for it, and

---

From the biographies of Filippo Brunelleschi and Giacomo della Porta in F. Milizia, *The Lives of Celebrated Architects, Ancient and Modern* . . . , translated from the Italian by Mrs. Edward Cresy, with notes and additional lives (London, 1826), I, 179ff. II, 89.

always recommended even in his last moments, that it should be built of heavy marble because, the cupola being raised on four arches, it would have a tendency to spring upwards, if not pressed with a heavy weight. . . . It is difficult to imagine why the cupola of Florence should have been so much thought of, when those of St. Sophie at Constantinople, of St. Mark in Venice, and of the Cathedral at Pisa, had already been executed. It is true that they are not double, and are supported by arches on four piers, whereas that of Brunelleschi is erected entirely on the walls and is octangular. What is particularly observable in the construction of this cupola, is, that there are no apparent [buttresses].

He also built a great part of the church of San Lorenzo at Florence, 259 feet long in the interior, and full of many errors, produced from envy or ignorance on the part of those who succeeded this able man. The pilasters on the steps have their bases higher than those of the columns, which are on the same level, a fault which might easily have been remedied by placing under the base of the columns a plinth sufficiently high to have come level with those of the pilasters. . . . From his time is fixed the epoch of the restoration of good architecture. . . .

In every age cupolas have been in use. . . . Those of Pisa have the disagreeable Gothic contour from which Brunelleschi has not departed very far in his celebrated cupola of the Cathedral of Florence, having placed one ingeniously within the other.

John Ruskin (1819–1900)
From *The Seven Lamps
of Architecture* (1849)

For architecture being in its perfection the earliest, as in its elements it is necessarily the first, of arts, will always precede, in any barbarous nation, the possession of the science necessary either for the obtaining or the management of iron. Its first existence and its earliest laws must, therefore, depend upon the use of materials accessible in quantity, and on the surface of the earth; that is to say, clay, wood, or stone: and as I think it cannot but be generally felt that one of the chief dignities of architecture is its historical use; and since the latter is partly dependent on consistency of style, it will be felt right to retain as far as may be, even in periods of more advanced science, the materials and principles of earlier ages.

But whether this be granted me or not . . . , it may perhaps be permitted to me to assume that true architecture does not admit iron as a constructive material, and that such works as the cast-iron central spire of Rouen Cathedral, or the iron roofs and pillars of our railway stations, and of some of our churches, are not architecture at all. Yet it is evident that metals may, and sometimes must, enter into the construction to a certain extent, as nails in wooden architecture, and therefore as legitimately rivets and solderings in stone; neither can we well deny to the Gothic architect the power of supporting statues, pinnacles, or traceries by iron bars; and if we grant this, I do not see how we can help allowing Brunelleschi his iron chain around the dome of Florence, or the builders of Salisbury their elaborate iron binding of the central tower. If, however, we would not fall into the

---

J. Ruskin, *The Seven Lamps of Architecture,* fourth ed. (Kent, 1883), Ch. II, "The Lamp of Truth," Sec. IX, X, pp. 40f.

old sophistry of the grains of corn and the heap, we must find a rule which may enable us to stop somewhere. This rule is, I think, that metals may be used as a *cement,* but not as a *support.*

Charles Herbert Moore

(1840–1930)

From *Character of Renaissance Architecture* (1905)

The great change in ideas and ideals which, after the remarkable intellectual and artistic life of the Middle Ages, was manifested in the so-called Renaissance, is not always correctly conceived or fairly stated; and the character and merits of the Fine Arts of the Renaissance, as compared with those of Medieval times, have not, I think, been often set forth in an entirely true light. Of the merits of the best Italian art of the fifteenth and sixteenth centuries there can be no question, but the belief that this art is altogether superior to that of the Middle Ages will not bear examination in the light of impartial comparison. . . . The Fine Arts of the Renaissance are in part a reflection of this decadent art of classic antiquity, and in part an expression of something quite different which was peculiar to the Italian genius at the time. To the man of the Renaissance the classic inspiration was necessarily different from what it had been to the man of antiquity. To the ancient Greek and Roman the pagan ideals had been real, and their inspiration was genuine, but to the Italian of the fifteenth century these ideals could not have the same meaning, or supply a true incentive. After the intervening centuries of Christian thought and experience, it was impossible for men to approach the ancient themes

C. H. Moore, *Character of Renaissance Architecture* (New York, 1905), from Ch. I ("Introduction"), pp. 1, 4, from Ch. II ("The Dome of Florence"), and Ch. III ("Church Architecture of the Florentine Renaissance"), pp. 22–30.

in the spirit of the ancients. Thus the neo-pagan art of the Renaissance is not wholly spontaneous and sincere. It contains elements that are foreign to the pagan spirit, and not compatible with it. The art of the Renaissance is in fact, an embodiment of heterogeneous ideas and conflicting aims.

• • •

The dome of Florence is indeed a remarkable piece of construction, and it is no less remarkable as a work of art. In beauty of outline it has not, I think, been approached by any of the later elevated domes of which it is the parent. Yet with all of its mechanical and artistic merit, the scheme is fundamentally false in principle, since it involves a departure from sound methods of dome construction. A bulging thin shell of masonry on a large scale cannot be made secure without abutment, much less can such a shell sustain the weight of a heavy stone structure like the lantern of this monument, without resort to the extraneous means of binding chains. A builder having proper regard for true principles of construction in stone masonry would not undertake such a work. For although it may be possible to give the dome a shape that will be measurably self-sustaining as to thrusts, as Brunelleschi clearly strove to do,[1] it is not possible to make it entirely so, and therefore if deprived of abutment it must be bound with chains. But a structure of masonry which depends for stability on binding chains is one of inherent weakness, and thus of false character.[2]

From these considerations it appears to me that Brunelleschi led the way in a wrong direction, notwithstanding the nobility of his achievement from many points of view. And in following his example

---

[1] In his explanation of his scheme before the Board of Works, as given by Vasari, Brunelleschi begins as follows: "Considerato le difficultà di questa fabbrica, magnifici Signori Operaj, trovo che non si può per nessun modo volgerla tonda perfetta, atteso che sarebbe tanto grande il piano di sopra, dove va la lanterna, che mettendovi peso rovinerebbe presto." [Vasari-Milanesi, Florence, 1880.—Ed.]

[2] It may be thought that this would condemn the use of metal clamps in masonry, such as were inserted in the walls of the Parthenon, or the wooden ties that were, in some cases, used in parts of Gothic buildings. But there is a wide difference between such use of clamps and ties, and the binding chains of the great domes of the Renaissance. In the Greek and Gothic work the masonry forms are favourable to stability independently of the clamps and ties. These were inserted either for security against unusual dangers, as from earthquakes, or for temporary security against rupture while the work was in progress, before the interaction of the parts of the system was fully established; but a dome without abutment violates the constant conditions of stability.

modern designers of elevated domes have wandered still farther, as we shall see, from the true path of monumental art.

Moreover, when we consider that a dome set within its drum is not only stronger, but that it is also much better for interior effect, the dome of the Pantheon still remaining the grandest and most impressive arched ceiling of its kind in the world, the unbuttressed modern domes, with their manifold extraneous and hidden devices for security, appear still less defensible.

But in the architectural thought of the Renaissance little heed was given to structural propriety or structural expression, and the Italian writers, who have largely shaped our modern architectural ideas, have not only failed to recognize the inherent weakness of such a building as the dome of Florence, but have even considered the work praiseworthy on account of those very characteristics which make it weak. Thus Sgrilli lauds Brunelleschi for having had the "hardihood to raise to such a height the greatest cupola which until its time had ever been seen, upon a base without any abutments, a thing that had not before been done by any one." [3] And Milizia says, "It is worthy of special notice that in the construction of this cupola there are no visible abutments." [4]

As to the permanent stability of this dome various opinions have been held by the experts among the older writers.[5] Its form is, as we have seen, as favourable to stability as it would be possible to make that of any vault which could be properly called a dome. It appears to the inexperienced eye as stable as a crest of the Apennines. Every precaution as to material and careful workmanship seems to have been taken to make it secure. The wall of the drum on which it rests is five metres in thickness, and the solid base of the dome itself is built, if the architect's scheme was carried out as he had stated it before the Board of Works, of large blocks of hard stone, thoroughly bonded and clamped with iron. The lower system is sufficiently strong, and appears to rest on a solid foundation. But nevertheless there are ruptures in various parts of the structure which have caused apprehensions of danger,[6] and its future duration must be regarded as un-

---

[3] *Discrizione e Studj dell' Insigne Fabbrica di S. Maria del Fiore,* Florence, 1733, p. xxi.

[4] *Memorie degli Architette,* etc., Florence, 1785, vol. I, p. 190.

[5] Fontana, Nelli, Cecchini, and others. [See note 6,—Ed.]

[6] These ruptures were first observed in the year 1693 (Nelli, *op. cit.,* [*Discorsi di Architettura,* Florence, 1753,—Ed.] p. 13), and it was then advised by the archi-

certain. The writers who have maintained that it is secure have argued on the assumption that the parts of a dome all tend toward the centre.[7] These writers overlook the fact that the force of gravity above, especially when the dome is heavily weighed by a lantern, neutralizes the inward tendency of the lower parts and causes a tendency in those parts to movement in the opposite direction. This neutralizing force is lessened by giving the dome a pointed form, as Brunelleschi has done, but, as before remarked, it can hardly be overcome entirely so long as any real dome shape is preserved.[8]

It may be thought that the object which Brunelleschi had in view, of producing a vast dome that should be an imposing feature of the cathedral externally, justifies the unsound method of construction to which he resorted (the only method by which the effect that he sought could be attained). But structural integrity is, I think, so fundamental a prerequisite of good architecture that in so far as this gifted Florentine was obliged to ignore sound principles of construction in order to attain an end not compatible with such principles, the result cannot be properly considered as an entirely noble and exemplary work of art, however much beauty and impressiveness it may have.

The example set by Brunelleschi was, in point of construction,

---

tect Carlo Fontana to add a new chain of iron. Nelli, however, argued that the fissures had not arisen from thrust, but were due to a slight yielding of the foundations, and he urged that no chain be added, but that a bit of marble be dove-tailed into the vault across the opening, in order that any further movement might be detected by the breaking of this marble. For three years no further sign of disturbance was noticed, but a slight earthquake in 1697 broke a portion of the masonry of the outer face of the dome opposite the fissure across which the marble had been placed. It appears, however, to have been concluded that there was still no danger from thrust, and no new chain was inserted. Cecchini (*Opinione intorno lo Stato della gran Cupola del Duomo di Firenze,* published together with Nelli's *Discorsi,* etc., p. 82) speaks of several cracks in both the inner and the outer shells of the vault, and also in the supporting piers, even down to the ground. But he agrees with Nelli in attributing these to movements of the foundations from which he concludes that no further danger is to be apprehended, and he affirms that the structure is entirely safe.
[7] Cf. Nelli, *op. cit.,* p. 73.
[8] The thrusts of a hemispherical dome are, in some degree, restrained by the binding of its continuous courses of masonry under compression, but this is not enough for security, as experience has shown; and in a polygonal dome, like Brunelleschi's, there is no such binding force, because there are no continuous circles of masonry.

a pernicious one, and bore fruit of a still more objectionable character in the works of other gifted men less scrupulous than he, and less endowed with mechanical ingenuity . . .

Though there is nothing whatever of classic Roman character in this great dome, the lantern which crowns it, built from Brunelleschi's design after his death, has classic details curiously mingled with mediæval forms. Its eight piers are adorned with fluted Corinthian pilasters surmounted by an entablature, while the jambs of the openings have engaged columns carrying arches beneath the entablature in ancient Roman fashion. From the entablature rises a low spire with finials set about its base, and flying buttresses, adorned with classic details, are set against the piers. None of the classic details have any true classic character, nor has the ornamental carving, with which the composition is enriched, any particular excellence either of design or execution. But these details are invisible from the ground, and in its general form and proportions the lantern makes an admirable crowning feature of this finest of Renaissance domes.

● ● ●

No other work by Brunelleschi is comparable in merit to the great dome of the Cathedral. None of his other opportunities were such as to call forth his best powers, which appear to have required great magnitude to bring them into full play. In his other works the influence of his Roman studies is more manifest, and his own genius is less apparent. In these other works he revives the use of the orders, and employs them in modes which for incongruity surpass anything that imperial Roman taste had devised. . . .

A particularly awkward result of this improper use of an order [in the interior of the Pazzi Chapel—Ed.] is that the entablature passes through the arch imposts, making an irrational structural combination. This scheme was, however, extensively followed in the subsequent architecture of the Renaissance, but it is a barbarism for which no authority, can, I believe, be found in ancient Roman design.[9]

---

[9] The entablature does, however, occur under vaulting in some provincial Roman buildings, as in the Pantheon of Baalbek. . . . But this, though not defensible, is less objectionable than the Renaissance scheme of an entablature passing through the imposts of archivolts.

Geoffrey Scott (1885–1929)
From *The Architecture
of Humanism* (1914)

But Renaissance architecture is a very unfortunate field for the exer-
cise of this kind of [evolutionary] criticism, for the reason, already
established, that it was an architecture of taste; an architecture, that
is to say, which was not left to develope itself at the blind suasion of
an evolutionary law. It cast off its immediate past and, by an act of
will, chose—and chose rightly—its own parentage. It scorned heredity;
and, if it sometimes reflected its environment, it also did much to
create it. It could change its course in mid-career; it was summoned
hither and thither at the bidding of individual wills. Brunelleschi, at
its birth, searching with Donatello among the ruins of Rome, could
undermine tradition. Michael Angelo, independent of the law as
Prometheus of Zeus, controlled its progress more surely than did any
principle of sequence. And the forces which he set loose, a later will
—Palladio's—could stem, and the eighteenth century revoke. Here was
no procession of ordered causes, but a pageant of adventures, a fan-
tastic masque of taste.

With what result for criticism? Because Renaissance architecture
fits ill into the evolutionary scheme, it is on every side upbraided.
Because its will was consciously self-guided, it is called capricious.
Because it fails to illustrate the usual lessons of architectural development, it is called unmeaning. Because there is no sequence; because
the terms are "unrelated"—or related not strictly, as in the older styles,

G. Scott, *The Architecture of Humanism, A Study in the History of Taste* (London: Constable and Company, Ltd., 1914), from Ch. VI, "The Biological Fallacy,"
pp. 170–79. Reprinted by permission of the publishers.

by "evolution"—the terms are *ipso facto* valueless and false. A certain kind of intellectual interest is frustrated: *therefore* æsthetic interest is void. This is the evolutionary fallacy in taste.

At its hands, as at the hands of the Romantic Fallacy, Renaissance architecture suffers by neglect and it suffers by misinterpretation. It suffers by neglect: the historian, committed to his formulas of sequence, is constrained to pass hurriedly by a style which fits them so ill and illustrates them so little. But it suffers also by misinterpretation, for that slight account of the Renaissance style which is vouchsafed is given, as best may be, in the formulas of the rest. It is drilled, with the most falsifying results, into the lowest common terms of an architectural evolution. The prejudice to taste is not merely that facts are studied rather than values; it is not merely that the least worthy facts are studied most, and that the stress falls rather on what is historially illuminating than on what is beautiful. The prejudice is more profound. For evolution was schooled in the study of biology; and historical criticism, when it deals in values at all, tends unconsciously to impose on architecture the values of biology. Renaissance architecture is blamed, in the general, because it is self-guided and "arbitrary"; yet it is condemned, in the particular, by the unjust dooms of "necessary" law. Let us take a typical presentation of the style, and see how this occurs.

The architecture of the Renaissance, we are told, and rightly, falls into three fairly distinct periods. There is the period of the Florentine Renaissance—the period of the *quattrocento*—tentative, experimental, hesitating, with a certain naïve quality that makes for charm but hardly for accomplishment: the period of which Brunelleschi is the outstanding figure. Of this manner of building the Pazzi Chapel is the earliest pure example, and the "Carceri" Church of Guiliano da Sangallo, at Prato, one of the latest. This is the period of immaturity.

The second period is that of Bramante and of Raphael. It is much more sure of itself; its aim is clearly defined and supremely achieved. The tentative Brunelleschian charm has vanished, and a more assured and authoritative manner has taken its place. Here, as at no other time, is struck a complete equipoise between majesty and refinement. The architecture of Bramante and Raphael and Peruzzi is as free from the childish and uncertain prettiness of the work which precedes it as from the "grossness and carelessness" of that which followed. . . .

It is a short period—a single generation well-nigh covers it. But it is the climax of the Renaissance and its prime. It synchronises with the climax of painting and civilisation. It is the architecture of Leo X and of Leonardo: the architecture of a time that could see its prototype in the assembled genius of the "School of Athens." This is the second period of Renaissance architecture: its supreme efflorescence.

And now begins the decline; the perfect equipoise could not be sustained. The inevitable decay sets in. It takes two complementary shapes: exaggeration and vacuity. The noble disposition of architectural forms gives place to restlessness: dignity is puffed into display. The sense of grandeur becomes the greed for size. It is the period of the Baroque: the period of decadence. The problem of style once solved—Bramante's school had solved it—nothing can remain but an abuse of power, and architecture feels the strain of too much liberty. . . .

Thus the third period of the Renaissance is marked sometimes by an opposite mood to its extravagance. The exquisite proportions of Raphael are hardened, in this decline, into academic formulas; architecture, when it is not ostentatious, becomes stiff, rigid, and inert. Simplicity becomes barren, and a restrained taste, vacant. And as the end draws near this vacancy is set in all finality on architecture's features by the Empire style. The Renaissance dies, its thoughts held fixed, by a kind of wandering memory, upon the classic past whence it arose, and which, in its last delusion, it believes itself to have become.

Such is the theme which, in their several manners, our histories repeat. But is it not too good, a little, to be true? Is it not a little like those stories of Herodotus that reveal too plainly the propensity of myth? This perfect image of the life of man—why should we look to find it in the history of architecture? This sequence of three terms— growth, maturity, decay—is the sequence of life as we see it in the organic world, and as we know it in ourselves. . . . Immaturity, prime, and decay follow one another in predestined sequence. Architecture is still presented to us as an organism with a life of its own, subject to the clockwork of inevitable fate. After Brunelleschi the herald, and Bramante the achiever, must come Bernini and the fall.

Let us retrace the biologic myth. The period of Brunelleschi is tentative and immature—unskilled, but charming. This is true, in a sense, but already it is not exactly true. It asks us to regard Brunelleschi's architecture as a less adept solution of Bramante's problem. It presents him as struggling with imperfect instruments after an ideal which later was fulfilled. We are bound to see his architecture in this light if our thoughts are on the *sequence*. In relation to the sequence, the description may be just. But this precisely was the fallacy of evolution. The values of art do not lie in the sequence but in the individual terms. To Brunelleschi there was no Bramante; his architecture was not Bramante's unachieved, but his own fulfilled. His purpose led to the purpose of Bramante: they were not on that account the same. There is in the architecture of the early Renaissance a typical intention, a desire to please, quite different from Bramante's monumental intention—his desire to ennoble. The immaturity of a child is spent in "endless imitation" of the maturer world, expressed with unskilled thoughts and undeveloped powers. But the "immaturity" of the Renaissance was rich with the accumulated skill of the mediæval crafts: it was in some directions—in decorative sculpture, for example—almost too accomplished. And it was not spent in feebly imitating the mature, for the obvious reason that the "mature" did not yet exist. True, the antique existed; but the Brunelleschian architecture was far from merely imitating the classic architecture of Rome. It had a scale of forms, a canon of proportions and an ideal of decoration that were all its own. The conception of immaturity, therefore, while it is appropriate in one or two respects, is in others misleading; and the parallel is so forced that it were best relinquished.

The first condition of æsthetic understanding is to place ourselves at the point of vision appropriate to the work of art: to judge it in its own terms. But its own terms will probably not be identical with those of the sequence as a whole. If we insist on regarding the sequence, we are forced to compare Brunelleschi with Bramante, and this can only be done in so far as their styles are commensurable—in so far as they have purposes in common. We shall compare them with regard to their command of architectural space and logical coherence, and here, no doubt, Brunelleschi is tentative and immature. But that does not exhaust his individuality: these qualities were not his total aim. The more stress, then, that we lay on the sequence the less justice shall we do to *quattrocento* architecture. The habit of regarding Brunelleschi simply as Bramante's precursor long allowed his genius to remain in shadow. Not so very long ago the assertion of his independent rights, his unrepeated merit, was received as a paradox. He came first in a long sequence, and "without experience"; how could he, therefore, be supremely great?

The evolutionary criticism which belittled the period of Brunelleschi—and from the same unconscious motive—was something more than just to the period of Bramante: the "prime and climax" of our architecture's life. Noble as it was in the hands of its finest architects, the central style of the Renaissance had, none the less, its vice. . . . It could be as vacant as the Empire Style, and as imitative as the spirit of life which, in spontaneous gaiety never fails to play upon the sunny architecture of the *quattrocento;* the life which in the *seicento* flowed out and gave itself in prodigal abundance to a thousand ventures; the life which had been smiling and later laughed aloud, flickers too often in these intervening years to a dim elusive spark.

Cornel von Fabriczy (1839–1910)

From *Filippo Brunelleschi,*
His Life and Work (1892)

Compared to Manetti's naive chronicle of Brunelleschi's life, which fundamentally puts the stress in the right places, Vasari's ac-

---

C. v. Fabriczy, *Filippo Brunelleschi, Sein Leben und Seine Werke,* Stuttgart, 1892, from Ch. II, 38–43. Translated by Renate Franciscono.

count—so far as it deviates from Manetti's, for it really only puts the same information in new trappings—is far less convincing. Vasari looks back upon Brunelleschi's historical personality from the vantage point of his own period, and ascribes to the time of Brunelleschi's [early] Roman studies fixed intentions and preconceived points of view that can only be abstracted from the master's total artistic achievement and personality. According to Vasari's account, Brunelleschi was guided from the start by two large ideas. First he wanted to revive the ancient art of building and thereby to assure his own immortality. Second, he was searching for a way to vault the dome of Santa Maria del Fiore. As far as the latter motive is concerned, it could not have figured in Filippo's first trip to Rome, since the project for the vaulting of the Cathedral lay still far in the future and the young artist could hardly have had such foresight and anticipation of future tasks and goals. This is not to deny, however, that as the dome project, which developed over the course of years alternately spent [by Brunelleschi] in Florence and Rome . . . was discussed more and more, it increasingly seized his imagination, and that his studies of comparable Roman monuments were partly responsible for the ripening in his mind of tangible ideas that he could later put into execution. We must be careful, however, not to ascribe too great an influence to the ancient models, especially the Pantheon, as Semper did for example. It is indeed because of the structural solution to the problem that they must be excluded from direct consideration. In the case of an octagonal cloister vault carried on piers, such as we have in the dome of Florence Cathedral but for which no example has been found in ancient Rome, the solution is based on a significantly different principle of statics than that used in true Roman domes erected over continuous buttressing walls. Thus . . . , the models for Brunelleschi's creation are less to be sought among these than among the circular and centralized buildings of the Middle Ages.

Brunelleschi's intention to revive the ancient art of building—*la buona architettura* Vasari calls it—must also be taken *cum grano salis*. The artists who stood at the threshold of the new age were not so clearly aware of a break with the ideas and forms of the past as the historical reflections of a later epoch would make it appear, caught as they were in the formalist spell of antiquity. They could no more give an abstract accounting for their relationship to ancient art than could the humanists for their relationship to ancient literature and culture. What they sought in the "rebirth" of ancient art was to familiarize themselves with the essence and forms of antiquity so that they could apply their knowledge independently and creatively to the problems of their own age. Only to the extent that antiquity could be made to serve these problems could it be revived; and only in this sense can the intention Vasari attributes to his hero be accepted. It cannot have been directed toward a conscious renewal of the entire organism of Roman architecture: the documents upon which such a renewal could have been based were too fragmentary, the general knowledge of antiquity too embryonic, and the artistic spirit of the times too devoted to personal creativity to make critically accurate reproductions. The initial steps in this direction taken soon afterward by Leon Battista Alberti under the impetus of the teachings of Vitruvius had not been pursued. Only when the creative impulse of the Early Renaissance had given way to the reflective spirit of the later period were they successfully taken up by the so-called Vitruvians of the cinquecento. It was not the organic unity of Roman architecture that the quattrocento architect sought and found in the ruins but the formal beauty manifest in its separate parts, in their relationship to one another, and especially in its richness of ornamentation. He freely used these elements to develop further and reshape problems that in the main were handed down from the Middle Ages. What earlier centuries had viewed with dull eyes—and had even tried at times to imitate with clumsy hands—was brought to new life by the fine formal sense of the Renaissance; and in return the creations of the new architecture were endowed with the most exquisite charm. But the Renaissance did not founder in the slavish imitation of its models— which the Middle Ages had to some extent attempted with so little success: its exuberantly youthful creativity enabled it independently to transform ancient structures and ornamentation, and by preserving the essence of antiquity to bring forth new artistic forms from the new elements. For in Burckhardt's words, "the Renaissance never treated antiquity as anything but the means of expressing its own architectural ideas; it used the antique only in the freest combinations."

In each of these aspects the pioneering architectural genius of Brunelleschi pointed the way for the new era; it is this which must be emphasized if we wish to determine *a posteriori* from the character of his architectural creations the nature of his Roman studies and their influence upon his work. With a single glance, keener than that of any artist before him, he grasped the essential difference between the character of antiquity and the art of the Middle Ages. How instructive it is in this connection to compare his formal language with that of his fellow pioneers of the early Renaissance, Piero di Giovanni, Niccolo di Piero, Nanni d'Antonio di Banco, yes, even Ghiberti and Donatello! With his essentially antique feeling for moderation, Brunelleschi stands as far above Donatello's often formless naturalism as above Ghiberti's smooth formalism. His knowledge of classical forms, based upon careful measurements and sketches, not only allowed him to imitate and reshape them with hitherto unexampled ease, it also fertilized his imagination to such a degree that his completely independent creations appear as if suffused with the spirit of antiquity.

How profoundly Brunelleschi understood the nature of ancient architecture can be gathered only imperfectly from his works. Whether he grasped the interrelationship of the columnar orders with the same acuity he did architectural details remains uncertain, since we have no example of their combined use in any of his executed buildings. That his attention was also caught by the groundplans of ancient monuments can be demonstrated in the single work [S. Maria degli Angeli] in which he was guided by a particular Roman model [Temple of Minerva Medica], though on that basis alone we can probably assume his interest in the plans of all Roman buildings as far as they were accessible to him. The fact that his other buildings show no direct dependence upon ancient groundplans is explained . . . in part by the specific circumstances of their creation, in part by their intended purposes. Otherwise, as A. Springer has rightly stressed [in *Bilder aus der Neuern Kunstgeschichte* (Bonn, 1886)], we have no evidence, direct or indirect, for any larger understanding by Brunelleschi of Roman architecture as an organism, for any comprehensive view of its creations in their totality. There is just as little evidence that he tried, as has been claimed, to learn the laws of proportion and spatial articulation in order to be able to explain architectural effects on the basis of specific numerical relationships. . . . What Manetti says in this connection about "musical proportions" was taken from the theories of Leon Battista Alberti a generation later.

Alberti himself, incidentally, declared that their effect was unmeasurable and that it could be evoked only by a developed artistic sensibility. It is just to this artistic sensibility and not to the repetition of proportions measured and explored in ancient monuments that the harmony of Brunelleschi's magnificent spatial conceptions will always have to be ascribed.

Finally, it remains to be pointed out that one of the most important aspects of [Brunelleschi's] Roman investigations concerns his study of the technical side of ancient architecture. His biographers have recorded that he was more qualified for it than many because of his thorough mathematical and mechanical knowledge, and that he was drawn to it by natural talent and predilection. Even were this not the case, his later astonishing technical achievements in building the Cathedral dome would be eloquent witness to how forcefully and successfully he was also able to use the technical lessons learned from the ancient monuments. . . . These studies led, sometime during the later years of his sojourn in Rome, to the project of the Florentine dome which in the course of time had been taking increasingly more tangible form. When Brunelleschi's biographers maintain that he kept his investigations and intentions for this project a carefully guarded secret even from Donatello, so that the credit for having mastered the problem would not be taken by others, they overlook the fact that Donatello left Rome after only about two years, at a time when Filippo could hardly yet have been thinking about the problem. They overlook still more the fact that the two artists . . . worked together on a model for the first competition for the Cathedral dome. Any secrecy about his studies is better explained, therefore, by the independent nature of Filippo's personality and his natural reserve; unless, indeed, this claim were simply an embellishment by his biographers invented to give their story a more personal cast.

Paolo Fontana (1865–1944)
From Brunelleschi and Classical
Architecture (1893)

[Authoritative critics have observed that] there is not a strict relationship between the classical and the Brunelleschian style in architectural
details; some of his profiles, in fact, display Gothic style, and the
proportions and ornamentation of his trabeation do not follow the
principles of antique art; even the style of his capitals departs re-
markably from antique standards. Brunelleschi as the presumed restorer of Roman architecture appears in reality to be its barely faithful
disciple. . . . An analysis of his works demonstrates that he con-
formed much more than is realized to earlier models found not in
Rome but in Florence or nearby cities.

Still standing today in Florence and its surroundings are some
Romanesque churches whose architects adopted classical forms with
more or less freedom: these are the Baptistery, SS. Aspostoli, San
Miniato, the portico of Sant'Iacopo, the facades of San Salvatore, the
Fiesolan Badia, and the Collegiata of Empoli. During the reign of
the Gothic style, Florentine architects did not completely neglect the
study of those structures. Brunelleschi, however, turned to them almost exclusively and, with the power of his genius initiated an architectural style which, in comparison with the then-prevalent Gothic,
could have seemed to be the resurgence of antique art. More than any
other building, the Baptistery of San Giovanni attracted his attention. There is an early tradition, still accepted today, that [the
Baptistery] was erected in a remote period for the cult of a pagan

The passages reprinted here are condensed from pages 258–260 and 264–266 of
P. Fontana, "Il Brunelleschi e l'architettura classica," in *Archivio Storico dell'Arte*,
6 (1893), 256–267. The translation from which this condensation was prepared
was made by Beverly Levine.

divinity and only later was consecrated to Christianity. In Brunelleschi's time nobody doubted this tradition, and cultured and uncultured alike admired the building as a monument of Roman architecture. Vasari puts words of great admiration for that temple in Filippo's mouth. In fact, Vasari himself had great admiration for the ancient structure, and exalted its merits in his biography of [Andrea] Tafi; and he also realized that the building had been held in no less esteem before his time. If Brunelleschi, therefore, considered the Florentine Baptistery ancient and beautiful, one must suppose even without having other proof that before going to study the ruins of Rome he would have studied lovingly all the parts of the Baptistery. A mention of such studies may be found, I believe, in the statement by Manetti about one of Brunelleschi's exercises in perspective: "And the first example demonstrating this principle of perspective was on a small plank approximately half a *braccia* square where he had made a drawing resembling the exterior of the Church of San Giovanni of Florence." But it is not really necessary to make great inductive efforts or to hoard bits of circumstantial evidence to establish that Brunelleschi studied the Baptistery. All his works give manifest proof that he not only studied the architectural parts of the noble building, but also took from them whatever might serve him for the adornment of his own works. . . .

Nor did Brunelleschi limit himself to the study of Florentine churches, but turned his attention to those of other Tuscan cities as well. Dehio has already noted that the Duomo in Pisa could have suggested to Brunelleschi the crossing in Santo Spirito; and Burckhardt sees corbels, like those used on one flank of San Frediano to sustain the cornice, throughout Filippo's work. This example is not unique; similarities can also be observed in other important churches in [Pisa, Pistoia, and Lucca.]

[Following a technical analysis of portions of Brunelleschi's architecture, Fontana concludes:]

I trust that my reasoning has sufficiently proved that Brunelleschi drew his beautiful style not from the ruins of Rome but from the monuments of Florence and other Tuscan cities. Aside from the proof of details, considerations of a general nature are also supportive. If Filippo drew and measured the ancient Roman structures over many long years, it is not only natural but necessary to assume that once he passed from study to implementation his great familiarity with classical forms would have led him, even without his willing it, to apply those forms to his own structures. No biographer's authority can make us forget that even genius begins by imitating, and only later finds itself strong enough to abandon the path marked by others in order to forge a new one. It is well known that Raphael, though gifted by nature with the most marvelous qualities, began by following in the tracks of his teachers so faithfully that even the most attentive observer could not have been certain whether some figures were by Raphael or his teacher. The same can be said of other artists; Brunelleschi alone should be exempt from this universal observation. He traveled, instead, in a totally opposite direction. In fact, in his early works the profiles of the mouldings and the capitals are further from classical excellence than in those works he executed when the effectiveness of his studies of antique architecture was no longer so strong, when his genius was more mature and consequently more adept at avoiding imitation. . . .

[Vasari's] authority so implanted the belief that Brunelleschi had learned by indefatigable study the art of construction at Rome, that even the most attentive observers viewed his work through a lens of prejudice. Milizia and d'Agincourt, following Vasari, admitted that the restorer of classical art had studied the Florentine Baptistery, but they gave infinitely greater importance to the effectiveness of the Roman models. Among more recent writers, some do note partial analogies between the works of [Brunelleschi] and the buildings of Tuscany, but without giving them the importance they merit. But my new observations should lead one to ask how much importance can be given to [Brunelleschi's] study of ancient structures. I do not wish to deny that the great architect went to Rome. . . . But his sojourn in Rome could not have been as lengthy as Manetti describes it, nor did Brunelleschi bring back with him that collection of [drawings] that others suppose when they place at the beginning of the architectural Renaissance not the true Brunelleschi but a Brunelleschi masquerading as Palladio. Filippo's [lengthy] sojourn in Rome, of which it should be noted no trace has been found in that city, is by itself unlikely; and the way it is narrated by Manetti, with so many details that we think his account an eyewitness report of that artistic expedition, has all the appearances of a piece of fiction.

My conclusions do not remove one laurel from the brilliant artist's crown. On the contrary, if he were to be considered merely the apprentice of the ancients he would remain greatly inferior, whereas if we believe that by studying imperfect structures he learned how to establish a new art, his worth increases in our minds.

Hans Folnesics (1887–1922)

From *Brunelleschi,*
a Contribution to the History
of the Development of Early
Renaissance Architecture (1915)

In his own day Brunelleschi was already considered the greatest architect since antiquity, and the chroniclers and writers of anecdotes who followed could not praise him enough as the great renewer who, with his Cathedral dome, surpassed the proud ancient model of the Pantheon and so brought to an end the despised style of the Middle Ages, the *rozzezza gotica.* The Florentine dome still represented the beginning of a new era for Burckhardt. Then suddenly new archival research produced quite unexpected results: it was not Brunelleschi's ardent spirit that had arched the outline of the dome against the sky with such infinite audacity; instead that outline had already been determined in a decision of 1367.[1] At first it must have come as a

---

H. Folnesics, *Brunelleschi, Ein Beitrag zur Entwicklungsgeschichte der Fruh-Renaissance Architektur* (Vienna, 1915), pp. 9–10, 97–99. Translated by Renate Franciscono.

[On this see F. D. Prager and G. Scaglia, *Brunelleschi, Studies of His Technology and Inventions* (Cambridge, Mass., 1971), pp. 2–9; and H. Saalman, "Santa Maria del Fiore: 1294–1418," *The Art Bulletin,* XLVI (1964), 487ff.— Ed.]

surprise that this work, traditionally accepted as the cornerstone of the new Renaissance architecture, should have been conceived and decided upon by Gothic masters. But closer observation does show, however, that the dome with its ogival section, the *quinto acuto*,[2] presents a completely Gothic line, that the distribution of weight to the eight corners by the ribs—the so-called *sproni*—follows a thoroughly Gothic structural principle, and finally, that clear antecedents for it are to be found in numerous domes over crossings and baptisteries. The analogy with the Pantheon which has been drawn time and again since Vasari,[3] rests entirely on their equal diameters, a correspondence that loses much of its significance because of the unequal height of the two buildings and the consequent difference in their proportions.

As the builder of the dome, Brunelleschi now seems merely the ingenious executor of a daring idea conceived by his predecessors. His own intellectual contributions are the bold construction of the dome without armature or scaffolding, the reinforcement of the double-shelled structure, and all the technical inventions that were required in order to vault the mighty choir of Santa Maria del Fiore. As a builder, he surpassed everything that had come before, but as an artist his hands were tied. He neither could nor was permitted to change anything in the original plan.

Nevertheless, later generations were correct in seeing in him the great renewer of Italian architecture; except that his greatest engineering feat, the dome, had nothing to do with his work as an artist. Only by looking at the buildings he created without influence, with free hands, can we get to know the artist. If we can also succeed in eliminating later additions to the original structures and, where they were not completed by the master himself, any changes in their original plans, we will have a real basis on which to judge the artist and his achievements.

[Following his technical analysis of Brunelleschi's buildings, Folnesics concludes:]

When we look over the life work of the master once more we have to admit that he took little, in fact almost nothing, directly from

---

[2] [*Quinto acuto* is a pointed arch with a radius of curvature which equals four-fifths of the diameter of its base.—Ed.]

[3] [Folnesics misinterprets Vasari here. See above, p. 76.—Ed.]

antiquity. On the other hand, we have evidence that he often borrowed from Proto-Renaissance [Tuscan Romanesque] buildings. But to seek the prerequisites of Brunelleschi's work solely in the Proto-Renaissance would be misleading, for Gothic art was not a foreign element within the development of Italian art which needed only to be removed for that development to resume its normal course. It was the necessary expression of a changed artistic volition and was as important a prerequisite for Brunelleschi's buildings as was the Proto-Renaissance. Yet even if we include the Gothic in our considerations, the Proto-Renaissance was only the pre-condition and not the why and wherefore of his style. Such a building as the Pazzi Chapel cannot be explained by finding models for consoles and moldings. Brunelleschi was open to ideas on construction and form . . . but the true and essential part of his work was created by him. The workings of genius are not explained by external circumstances; their explanation lies within. In the essay [by Paola Fontana⁴ Brunelleschi is] compared to Raphael, who in his youth so closely imitated the styles of Perugino and Pinturicchio that many of the figures in the works he painted then cannot positively be identified as his, but who later far surpassed the artists he imitated. Fontana drew the comparison with the intention of honoring Brunelleschi, but it seems to me that he accomplished the opposite. For Raphael was perhaps the greatest learner of all time. He brought the sentimental sweetness of his first teacher, Perugino, to its ultimate expression, developed his skill in constructing great compositions under the influence of Fra Bartolomeo in Florence, and finally arrived at his *maniera grande* in contemplating the work of Michelangelo at Rome. In the process his development ran an unparalleled course; but he always needed someone to follow, even though in each case he finally surpassed him.

Not so Brunelleschi. He had no teacher; he created his first work in deliberate opposition to everything that had come before. Even if he himself also believed he was reviving the art of the ancients, what he created was in fact new. In this he can be said to resemble Columbus who thought he had reached the west coast of India when he discovered America. In comparison to Raphael's development, Brunelleschi's looks meagre. What he gave the world was so utterly new that he could not go beyond it at once; he first had to work it through,

⁴ [Folnesics has misread Fontana. See above, p. 103.—Ed.]

and to this task he dedicated his entire life. His buildings for this reason form a series like links in a chain; each is an advance over the preceding and inconceivable without it. This is also why each has its own inevitable place; it would be quite impossible to exclude any from consideration. Is there a single work of Raphael's, in contrast, that could similarly destroy our understanding, not only of his later development but of all future painting, if it were struck from his oeuvre? Raphael was one of the greatest sons of the Renaissance, but Brunelleschi was its father. For there would have been no Raphael without the Renaissance which came before him, but without Brunelleschi there would have been no Renaissance.

Ludwig Heinrich Heydenreich
From *The Late Works of
Brunelleschi* (1931)

"I have not been successful in ascertaining whether a development took place in Brunelleschi's style comparable to what we call Bramante's *ultima maniera*; a maniera that would anticipate in part the advances that we find in the works of the masters of the following generation which I am tempted to describe as the period of Alberti and Desiderio."

Nothing is more typical of the approach of the Burckhardt generation to the question of a development of Brunelleschi's style than this resigned acknowledgement by Geymüller.[1] For a writing of

L. H. Heydenreich, "Spatwerke Brunelleschis," in *Jahrbuch der Preuszischen Kunstsammlungen*, 52 (1931), 1–28. Illustrations from the original article have not been reproduced, but see Figs. 7, 8, 9, 13, 15–24 for relevant illustrative material.

[1] Stegmann-Geymüller, *Die Architektur der Renaissance in Toskana*, Vol. I, [1885–1893] *Text*, p. 66. Cf. also a similar passage in Vol. XIb, *General Survey*, p. 6.

history which presented Brunelleschi as the revolutionary genius and conscious innovator who manifested the new style immediately from his very first works, the whole oeuvre of this artist had necessarily to appear too unified for the treatment of a stylistic process *within* that oeuvre to find much place. For so long as Brunelleschi was being presented as the creative genius, the first exponent of an "individual style," his stylistic development could be treated—if at all—only from the standpoint of an examination of his vocabulary, especially in its details and decorative forms, for changes which could form the transition to similar motives in the individual forms of the architure of the next period, i.e. of the period of Alberti and Desiderio.

Over against this method of treatment, which is common to the works of Burckhardt, Geymüller, and Fabriczy,[2] the later interpretations (for which the very point of departure of the Burckhardt generation—that apparently so clear and certain concept of the Renaissance —became a problem in itself), subordinated the work of Brunelleschi completely to the Renaissance-Gothic problem. It is possible to follow almost step by step the formulation of the "synthetic" character of Brunelleschi's style (Fontana, Geymüller, Patzak, Frankl, Willich, Folnesics, and—published somewhat belatedly—Schmarsow).[3] The question of period style (*Zeitstil*) is paramount throughout. Brunelleschi is seen as the mediator between two style phases; but the question of the characteristic expression of this transition, recognizable in a gradual freeing or at least changing process within the oeuvre of Brunelleschi—this question is again left unanswered, this time for the opposite reasons from those of the earlier generation.

Not until Dvořák and Dagobert Frey do we find approaches to such a statement of the problem. Dvořák[4] follows out for the first

[2] J. Burckhardt, *Geschichte der Renaissance*, 3rd ed. (1891), esp. p. 34; Geymüller, *op. cit.*; C. v. Fabriczy, *Brunellesco* (1892).

[3] P. Fontana in *Archivio storico d'arte*, VI (1893), 265ff. H. v. Geymüller, *Friedrich II von Hohenstaufen und die Anfänge der Architektur der Renaissance in Italien* (Munich), 1908. P. Frankl, *Die Renaissance-Architektur in Italien* (Leipzig, 1912). H. Willich, *Baukunst der Renaissance in Italien*, Vol. I (1914) (*Handbuch für Kunstwissenschaft*). H. Folnesics, *Brunelleschi* (Vienna, 1915) (compare with this Frankl's discussion in *Repertorium für Kunstwissenschaft*, 41 [1919], p. 225). Aug. Schmarsow, *Gotik in der Renaissance* (Stuttgart, 1921).

[4] M. Dvořák, *Geschichte der italienischen Kunst im Zeitalter der Renaissance, Akademische Vorlesungen*, Vol. I (Munich, 1927), 62ff. (esp. pp. 68 and 73ff.).

time a stylistic development within the works of Brunelleschi, in that by opposing the "static spatial volume" (*ruhender Baumkörper*) of the Renaissance to the Gothic "dynamic structure" (*Bewegungsbau*), he recognizes in him the development toward a *new* architectural style in the interplay between the purely "spatial" Gothic-medieval and the "plastic" antique conceptions of architecture. It may be because of his brief treatment of the theme that Dvořák does not entirely carry through these ideas, and does not go into the decisive significance of the late works in this development, but stops at the Pazzi Chapel, where he sees, for the first time—and quite rightly— this "plastic feeling" connected with the space realization, but where he also sees the "accomplishment of the genesis of the new style." Perhaps, on the other hand, the explanation for this interpretation can also be found in the no longer tenable premise for this development of Brunelleschi, the idea that the main inspiration for the formation of a new style was to be found in the artist's first trip to Rome.

Finally, Dagobert Frey, taking Dvořák as a point of departure, tried to give a new formulation to the stylistic progression in architecture from the Early Renaissance to the early cinquecento, in terms of the "development from hollow to plastic space" (*vom Hohlraum zum Körperraum*). It is interesting in this connection for our discussion that although Frey considers that the decisive shift to "plastic space" is achieved only about 1500, he observes already in Brunelleschi's late work, S. Spirito, a step in the direction of this development by comparison with the early work of S. Lorenzo; and thus he goes beyond Dvořák in suggesting a characterization of a late phase of Brunelleschi's style.[5]

From these various interpretations of Brunelleschi's oeuvre, which are yet so logically conditioned in their sequence, the problem which concerns us emerges clearly—i.e., the peculiar double aspect of Brunelleschi in respect to period style (*Zeitstil*) and individual style (*Individualstil*). In the process of distinguishing among the works of Brunelleschi, we must search for the shift from period style to individual style, and it will be our task to define the characteristic and decisive stages of this process in the development of his style. In

[5] Dagobert Frey, *Bramantes St.-Peter-Entwurf und seine Apokryphen* (Vienna, 1915). *Idem.*, *Architettura della Rinascenza* (Rome, 1924). *Idem.*, *Gotik und Renaissance* (Augsburg, 1929), esp. pp. 15–16, 105, 106.

the presentation of this problem the "late works" of the artist have a special significance, and form a coherent group whose general stylistic principle determined the direction of the development of Renaissance architecture to the "classic style."

• • •

From Burckhardt to Dvořák, the Pazzi Chapel has always been regarded as the clearest embodiment of Brunelleschi's ideas, and thus as the climax of his creative activity. All the characteristics of the new style seem to appear there in their clearest form; all Brunelleschi's experiments in his earlier works seem to have been thought through and conclusively formulated here: the spatial organization as the first experiment in a central type, the complete tectonic definition of the space, the clear proportions governed by the law of the "golden section," the perfection of the decorative forms, and finally the adoption of (antique) plastic sense in the definition of space.

The stylistic coherence of the first group of Brunelleschi's works —i.e. the Ospedale (begun 1419), the Old Sacristy (begun 1420), S. Lorenzo (begun 1421), and the Pazzi Chapel (begun 1429)—is so great that Fabriczy and Geymüller can find no bridge from the Pazzi Chapel to the late works of the master, and try to explain all apparent discrepancies in style as a result of hindrances to the artist from lack of funds (S. Maria degli Angeli) or of subsequent changes by the followers of Brunelleschi;[6] while more recent interpretations entirely ignore this question.[7]

As a matter of fact, in the works following the Pazzi Chapel a building style is begun which is so completely different from the preceding one that one might be tempted to speak not simply of a stylistic *development* but of a stylistic *reversal*. This applies to the following buildings which we wish to group together as late works from this point of view: the churches of S. Maria degli Angeli and S. Spirito, and beyond these the Lantern and the so-called Exedras of the Florentine Cathedral.

First let us present the first work of this group, the central building of S. Maria degli Angeli, which Brunelleschi constructed to

---

[6] Geymüller, *Toskanawerk*, Vol. I, *Text*, p. 67, and *passim*. Fabriczy, *op. cit.*, pp. 244, 207, 138.

[7] More detailed remarks will be given in the discussion of the various buildings.

its present height in the years 1434–37.[8] The deflection of the money allotted for the building to war expenses is known to have brought the work to an end, so that this most remarkable creation of the Early Renaissance has come down to us as only a torso.

A comparison of the various old descriptions of Brunelleschi's sketch (lost since about 1880) shows that we can consider the engraving after the original Brunelleschi drawing (published by Lastri in the *Osservatore Fiorentino* in 1821) as a copy which is faithful down to the last detail. Thus we gain at least an idea of the plan for this building which was of the greatest importance for the development of the central building of the Renaissance.

Brunelleschi gave the Angeli an architectural form which, in comparison with his earlier works, demonstrates a complete difference in architectural thinking: that form is *pier construction (Pfeilerkonstruktion)*.

Brunelleschi's earlier buildings are *wall* buildings; i.e. the tangible mass, the wall, is merely a space-enclosing shell, without any space-moulding function. One may conceive the construction of the Pazzi Chapel completely in terms of the wall and its decorative membering which clarifies the articulation of the building. Even though this membering is much more plastic than that of the Old Sacristy, this intensification is still within the limits of the same basic conception of the building in terms of wall that he had employed before, since it has to do primarily with the form of the details without encroaching on the essential nature of the building. In contrast, the Angeli is conceived entirely in terms of *mass*, for the eight subordinate spaces (the chapels) appear almost as if hollowed into the strong outer wall which surrounds the principal space, so that the three-cornered piers are to be thought of as the remaining pieces of the wall mass. This definition should not be interpreted to mean that Brunelleschi's space design went through this process; rather Brunelleschi probably first established the spatial layout here in much the same way that Leonardo later proceeded in drawing his sketches of central buildings. But what is characteristic and new is the fact that in this construction the tangible mass achieves a much stronger emphasis. The difference is that the function of merely bounding and

[8] Building history: Fabriczy, *op. cit.*, pp. 234ff.

enclosing the space is no longer sufficient for the wall mass, but that this wall mass is worked *into* and therefore worked *with;* the intrusion of niches from the inside and outside brings out a *plastic* quality in the tectonic modelling of the wall, which gives the wall mass independence and vitality within the building organism. It now becomes a factor of equal weight with the space design; it becomes a *space-moulding mass.*

The pier building in this form is antique (Pantheon, Minerva Medica); its revival, as Brunelleschi carried it out in the Angeli, means a turning away from Gothic tradition—and this is the decisive action in regard to the development of Brunelleschi. The same change appears in the elevation of the Angeli, with its heavy forms: the double pilasters of the inner corners, which appear here for the first time (instead of the earlier simple bent ones), and especially the technique of vaulting the dome which, as is apparent from the drawing, was to have been executed like the dome of the Pantheon and of Minerva Medica, in massive masonry (semicircular!). Also striking are the powerful profiles on framing mouldings, socles, and entablatures: here for the first time is established the beginning of a "plastic" feeling in the sense of an understanding of the mutual dependence of basic structural design and decorative membering. The heaviness and simplicity of the archivolt can be explained only as the result of a conscious attempt to assimilate the profile to the massiveness of the whole building: it takes in the whole width of the frame in a single strong projection, and no longer, as in earlier buildings, forms simply a border to it. Even though there is a definite antiquizing quality in this form, however, Brunelleschi's medieval thinking betrays itself in the general interpretation of the decorative forms. For a structural connection between the decoration and the essential design of the building has not yet been created. This is indicated by the neglect of the tectonic function of the decorative forms, for example when the continuous framing moulding of the niches is also the border to the chapel openings (being thus turned, to run around them), so that the door seems almost to have been shoved up into the border from below; and the same trait is shown on the exterior, where the framing mouldings of the eight sides are to be interpreted as running around them, running across the corner piers to right and left, under the entablature (which is supported by the piers) and on the socle below.

On the whole, however, the Angeli signifies a turning point in Brunelleschi's style; but the change is basic because it has to do no longer with merely the external features of the space design or the decorative forms, but with the interpretation of the total organism of the structure itself: in the Angeli Brunelleschi created the first pier building, and thus the first mass structure of the Renaissance.

If we inquire into the external and internal bases of this change in style, as it reveals itself in the Angeli, the building itself gives the first answer. It is obvious that the plan of this "bizarissimo tempio" could not have originated from Brunelleschi's own imagination alone . . . ; the architectural form of the Angeli is simply "uninventable" both as space design and in its whole structural form. We cannot find a direct prototype; the Pantheon and the Minerva Medica can be reckoned as indirect prototypes, since from them could originate antique space designs which may have given rise to the Angeli. That such ancient monuments did exist may be deduced from the central plans which have come down to us in the drawings of the Renaissance architects and in Montfauçon, and also from Roman tomb buildings.

It seems difficult at first to find a possible point of contact between Brunelleschi and such antique buildings. To link that contact with the legendary "first trip to Rome," before the beginning of his career as an architect, is impossible in view of the style of his early works, especially the Innocenti and the Old Sacristy. Therefore we are again forced back to the problem of the second trip to Rome, the calling of Brunelleschi to Rome by Pope Eugenius IV. . . . Manifold connections between Eugenius and Brunelleschi seem to speak very strongly for the fact that the latter was actually briefly in the service of the Pope [ca. 1433–34], especially since the lack of Florentine documents confirms his absence from Florence.

[However], we may not under any circumstances regard the Angeli as an exact "copy" of a Roman round building. What especially struck Bruneslleschi, as an already experienced architect, in Rome, must on the whole have been less the "canon" of antique monuments —on the basis of a systematic "study"—than the much more general recognition of the heavy, massive, "plastic" antique manner of building, a recognition for which the conditions lay already in his own line of development. For real theoretical examinations, measurements, and studies of proportions, even this second Roman trip was too early from the standpoint of the historical development: the image of the antique was still a too general one, especially since Vitruvius, who gave true impetus to these "archeological" studies and to the search for the antique "canon," was still completely unknown. (Even Alberti had not yet begun his architectural studies at this time.) It is true that from now on details appear in Brunelleschi's work which, in their sharper execution, in the use of ornamented fasciae in the entablature, especially, however, in their greater plasticity, confirm the idea of Roman influence (especially in the Lantern and in the Aedicules of the Cathedral), but the decisive element is to be found in the perception of that "massiveness," and in the use of the ancient "mass structure," which characterize his work from now on. . . .

Brunelleschi's two basilicas, S. Lorenzo and S. Spirito, stand in the same relation to each other as the Pazzi Chapel and S. Maria degli Angeli. In S. Lorenzo the space is enclosed by a pure *wall* architecture, with flat decorative membering. This "planarity" is especially obvious in the partition walls of the first two bays after the crossing, which remain from the original plan without chapels. Yet the wall-like character is preserved also in the later widening by the addition of side chapels; one may even say it is underlined: if one observes the profile of the transverse walls of the chapels, the openings seem to be cut out of the wall, and the thin transverse walls which divide each chapel from the next are drawn between the new outer wall and the remnants of the partition wall. . . .

In S. Spirito we find completely changed space proportions: arcades and upper story have the proportion of 1:1; that is, the crowns of the arches are at the mid-point of the nave height. Thus the height of the arcades in proportion to the total space is drastically reduced by comparison with those of S. Lorenzo (5:3). Now since, in spite of the proportional reduction of the span of the arches, the columns have the same height as those of S. Lorenzo, and are in addition more squat and heavier, they are much closer together in their sequence than is the case in S. Lorenzo. With the addition of the high upper story, therefore, the space impression is much more closed (i.e. more limited); the nave is conceived more as a spatial unit, beside which the aisles run as independent space corridors. Thereby the tendency toward tectonic spatial division is given still greater weight: the consistent proportion of 1:2 between the smaller and the next greater space units is still more clearly stated, and the organic structure of the building still more stressed. The reasoned coordination of space and mass design comes out in the measurements as compared to those of S. Lorenzo, down to the last detail, and it is apparent from them that the plan of S. Spirito (although it is also quite geometric in its logic) was designed with the thickness of the wall included in the calculations:[9] in this connection the feeling for "spatial plasticity" in the niche architecture of the outer wall takes on special stress. Instead of the "pierced wall" of S. Lorenzo, we find in S. Spirito separate piers between which extend the semi-circular niches. At the same time, with the aid of the oblique profiles (which, by the way, manifest the heavy archivolts of the Angeli, but doubled) a transition between pier and niche is created which draws the two together into an organic unity and obliterates the impression of an attached extrusion. The "space-bounding wall shell" of S. Lorenzo is thus replaced by a "space-moulding wall structure." This means, therefore, that here as in the Angeli the "tangible mass" now possesses a space-moulding function; it has attained an independent volume. The plastic feeling in the architectural design has penetrated so far that space and mass become factors of equal weight in the creation of a space design. In this manner also the "plastic" half columns, which are here set against the piers in place of the decorative pilasters in S. Lorenzo, take on a special meaning: they not only stress the structural function of the pier in the building organism, but they heighten, furthermore, by their sequence, the impression of the aisles as distinct spaces.

On this basis we can understand what importance should be attached to the fact that this ring of outer chapels was not planned from the beginning, but that Brunelleschi added them only later, thereby departing from his original building scheme. No one so far has correctly evaluated the previously mentioned fragment of the Manetti Vita discovered and published by Chiappelli, although it goes

[9] Cf. Folnesics, *op. cit.*, p. 74 and Dag. Frey, *Gotik und Renaissance*, p. 16.

beyond the other preserved manuscripts and contains just that part, which has always been so painfully missed, treating the building of S. Spirito.[10] In it we find the following decisive statement: "And when Filippo had made the model, and part [of the church] had been begun, at some point he said these words: that it seemed to him that he had begun a building that in respect to its composition was in accordance with his intentions. Certainly it did not depart from his model. He began it and founded some chapels and built a part of it in his time in accordance with that intention. It was beautiful, and with the material projecting toward the exterior had no equal in Christendom." This concerns the ring of chapels known also from other sources (whose original form, projecting also on the outside, is still visible today under the later walling up), which is here described as a subsequent change in plan by Brunelleschi. But this very widening produces a complete transformation in the building; in the first project it must be imagined with a straight enclosing wall, having its present form on the exterior, and thus similar to that of S. Lorenzo. With the addition of the chapels and of the changed pier construction which they condition, however, the plastic spatial effect on the interior that we have been discussing was brought out, while the plane of the exterior elevation is vitalized by the constant alternation of convex protrusions and the narrow, straight connecting walls; and this gives the wall a more plastic impression by its characteristic protrusions. For as on the interior pier and niche are drawn together into a unified design by the strong profiles, so also on the exterior the cornice running around the building (at the height of the springing of the chapel vaults) underlines the coherence of wall and niche.[11] The ring of chapels, and the cornice drawn like a ring around the whole building, also bring out with special clarity on the exterior the peripheral movement around the central point of the crossing, and make this building, with its "centralized basilica" form pursued with such pure and relentless logic, appear as a solution that in every respect presents a reasoned conclusion to the problem of S. Lorenzo.

---

[10] Ed. Chiappelli (1905), pp. 180, 181. Even Fabriczy, who discussed Chiappelli's edition in the *Repertorium für Kunstwissenschaft*, 20 (1897), p. 42, overlooked this passage.

[11] This entablature is still visible in the spaces still accessible between the various chapels and the present exterior wall (cf. Geymüller, *op. cit.*, p. 30).

Beyond the general space composition, the character of this widening of the plan of S. Spirito takes on special meaning in our presentation of the problem, because of the date of this change, . . . [which probably] took place probably between 1436 and 1439, [bringing] us to the second half of the thirties; that is to say, to the time immediately after the building of the Angeli. This clarifies, without further explanation, the essential connection in building form between the Angeli and S. Spirito: by the change in the plan of S. Spirito, Brunelleschi adapted the principle of "mass structure," which he had employed for the first time in the Angeli, to a basilican church. . . .

The building of the Angeli, on the whole a new invention, opened for Brunelleschi the possibility of extensive use of antique prototypes. Yet we must not—as has already been emphasized—see in it the first "copy" of an antique building, but rather the first "taking over" of the antique plastic and tangible conception of the building organism as a whole. In S. Spirito Brunelleschi adapted the principle of the pier construction—of the mass structure—to the medieval scheme of the longitudinal church. This adaptation, however, signifies a true "synthesis": in its inherited tradition and antique forms have interpenetrated to form a new unity.

• • •

The Aedicules (or Exedras) of the Cathedral of Florence, for which Brunelleschi delivered the model in 1438, and the first of which was finished in 1444,[12] are also plastically conceived massive constructions. Since no spatial requirements confronted him, but only that of a decorative structure, only the exterior form is treated: niches are let into the very strong and heavy walls, a repetition of the motif used for the first time on the Angeli, but here extended so that the niches now occupy the entire height of the wall. For the first time in the Renaissance, half columns appear here on the exterior (the façade of S. Spirito, which was to have had them, was never executed). The fact that they appear immediately in pairs, so that each niche is given its own pair of framing columns, shows especially clearly the plastic sense and also the sense of organic structural coherence in this architecture. It is interesting from this viewpoint that a first model for the Aedicules

---

[12] Documents in Fabriczy, *Brunellesco,* p. 137; and *Jahrbuch der Preuszischen Kunstsammlungen,* XXVIII (1907), Beiheft, p. 20.

shows no half columns, but rather "pilasters following the corner," as is evident from the documents (cf. note 12). In this first form, therefore, the Aedicules with corner piers would have been still more similar to the exterior of the Angeli. In the substitution of coupled half columns for the pilasters, however, the plastic feeling that strives toward structural clarity is expressed with particular clarity. The heavy and elaborate forms of the entablature and of the moulding profiles—again the same as those of the Angeli—also testify to this.

The high socle that raises the structure over the balustrade which runs around the whole Cathedral, and the elongated capitals of the Aedicules seem to speak for the fact that in the design their height above the ground was taken into account, and thus also the optical effect, that is, the danger of too strong foreshortening, was taken into consideration. One is tempted to accept this apparently purely hypothetical assumption in order to find an explanation for the strange stilt blocks between capital and entablature, which have an inner logic in the arcades of the church but are here entirely without structural motive. In addition they are not completely developed pieces of entablature, as in Brunelleschi's basilicas, but much flatter, so that they have perhaps been inserted with the intention of clearly setting off columns from entablature in order to avoid an optical confusion, which actually in a certain sense seems to have been achieved when they are viewed from the ground. Were this really the case, then the first beginnings of a new architectural problem would be discernible here: the inclusion of optics in the architectural design, whereby over and above the building's general "comprehensibility," the consciousness of the spectator's position in relation to the space and the mass of the building would be expressed. Now this assimilation of the perspective effect is in no way a phenomenon foreign to this period—it finds its theoretical definition only a few years later in Alberti, who states that a barrel vault should be raised as much as the cornice projection at the springing conceals it. It is rather merely a logical consequence, one might say a practical application, of the principle of making the space (and especially the building mass) comprehensible. An architectural concept which designs space "consciously" must necessarily try to achieve its harmonious effect also by reinforcing, by the *manner* of the design, the human capacity for seeing and understanding. Our belief that we can recognize the first beginnings of this effort in the works of Brunelleschi finds its support not only in the formation of details in the Aedicules which obviously correct the perspective effect, but also to a much stronger degree in the development of Brunelleschi's dome designs. For any architect who "consciously" designs in space, the reconciliation of interior and exterior impression becomes an important aesthetic problem in the design of a dome—and especially that of a crossing dome. The semicircular dome over the inscribed circle forms the most satisfying terminus to the block of space which it crowns on the interior; but its success on the exterior is spoiled as soon as a large building mass interferes with its visibility from below (e.g. S. Paolo a Ripa, Pisa). To avoid this discrepancy, Brunelleschi undertook three different experiments in his dome designs of S. Lorenzo, the Pazzi Chapel, and S. Spirito; in their rising development toward the most complete solution of the problem these furnish internal evidence of the presence of that problem.[13]

The dome of S. Lorenzo shows the most primitive form, which rests directly on the pendentives and is covered on the exterior by a form like a truncated rectangular tower with a pitched roof. In this way the problem is almost completely avoided, since the expression of the dome forms on the exterior is renounced. At the Pazzi Chapel the truncated tower on the exterior is cylindrical in form, and terminated by a conical roof. As a technical construction, this form comes very close to a second, outer dome shell raised higher than the inner one, as is especially evident in the cross-section. In S. Spirito,[14] finally, a small drum is inserted between pendentives and dome, narrow enough not to interfere with the interior effect, but sufficient to raise the dome on the exterior above the roof zone. But beyond this, and alongside this, is carried out the idea which was already present in germ in the dome of the Pazzi Chapel, an exterior raised shell being set over the inner

---

[13] Even if only the dome of the Pazzi Chapel was still executed under Brunelleschi's personal direction, the dome of S. Spirito is constructed throughout in the spirit of the Brunelleschi model (with the exception of the much later lantern), as is evident from the well-known letter of Dom. da Gaioles (cf. Gaye, *Carteggio*, I, 167). And in our opinion the frequently criticized mistakes in the dome of S. Lorenzo can also have to do only with clumsiness of the technical execution, but not with a deviation from the original form and construction of the Brunelleschi model (cf. Fabriczy, *op. cit.*, pp. 165ff.).

[14] Illustration of the section in Willich, *op. cit.*, I, 28 (Pazzi Chapel); and Laspeyres, *Kirchen der Renaissance in Mittelitalien* (Berlin and Stuttgart, 1882), p. 8 (S. Spirito).

dome, so that the dome in this form can hold its own better against the total mass of the building, and can also give it a worthy climax on the exterior. This last form, indeed, presents the most complete solution of the problem; above and beyond its direct imitation by Sangallo in the dome of the sacristy of S. Spirito, the drum and raised outer shell constitute from now on the basic elements of dome design in the Renaissance.

The hypothesis of a possible perspective construction in the Aedicules gains greater plausibility from the continuous development of the "optical" problem in Brunelleschi's dome solutions, especially since similar principles of design are discernible in the Lantern of the Cathedral, the artist's last work.

The Lantern of the Cathedral of Florence, the model for which was completed in 1436, and whose execution was begun in 1446 after many years of preparation of the material, fits in as a characteristic mass structure of Brunelleschi's late style by virtue of the heaviness of its forms, the half columns inserted between the main piers, the design of the pier buttresses in the form of a portal supporting volutes, and the double pilasters separated on the interior but unified on the exterior. . . . The plastic feeling for the building mass, however, is the real "antique" element, and thus Brunelleschi achieves in the Lantern the transformation of an originally Gothic rib construction into a basically antique peripteros monument.

The kind of lantern which Brunelleschi created has no prototype in architecture. Medieval lantern constructions, which are very numerous, always have the form of a simple round aedicule (e.g. Baptistery, Florence), which Brunelleschi himself had used in his lanterns for the Old Sacristy and the Pazzi Chapel. This form is also kept in Gothic buildings, and adapted to the style only in the form of the pointed arches (Pistoia Baptistery, Siena Cathedral). The use of buttressing arches in the Lantern, which give such a wonderful conclusion to the ribs of the dome, is Brunelleschi's own invention. The search for a related form leads, interestingly enough, to Italian goldsmith work of the late Gothic and early Renaissance, in which the tabernacle with flying buttresses is a form used extremely frequently for monstrances, holy vessels, and ornaments on bishops' staffs. . . .

The use of a similar tabernacle form in monumental architecture indicates the basic conception of the Cathedral Lantern as a crowning "ornament"; but the fusing of the formal concept with that antique plastic feeling for mass in architectural design gives this ornament a new form and content—in that it becomes a monument structure.

With the Lantern Brunelleschi also introduces the *volute* into architecture as a structural member: from here Alberti and Baccio d'Agnolo take the motive that becomes an important factor for façade and tower designs in the new architecture. Just this creation of the architectonic volute, however, is a characteristic contribution of the mature Brunelleschi: for this action is the exploitation of an ancient motif for the building requirements of his own time. Without doubt the form of the volute is derived from the antique console, and in this process of change the "style-creating" power of Brunelleschi again shows itself, the assimilation of antique formal tradition to the aims of the new style. For the volute, in its function as intermediate member between vertical and horizontal, finds its source, in respect to its expression of statics as well as to its aesthetic character, in the console. The console similarly forms a structural transition between two parts of a building at right angles to each other and in its form not only expresses this transition "functionally" (by its tension) but also softens it "aesthetically" (by its flowing movement).

Even if only the base of the Lantern was executed under Brunelleschi's personal direction, nevertheless the form and structure of the whole construction are entirely his own creation. Here too we must recognize the concern with optical effect, in the stilting of the arched window frames, in the strong protrusion of the entablature and the exceedingly sharp working of the details (egg and dart moulding). It is the high position of the Lantern that necessitates special concern for optical effects within the structure.

On the whole, the Lantern of the Cathedral, the artist's last work, shows in its purest form the solution of the problem which underlay Brunelleschi's life work: to find a synthesis between heritage and antiquity, and with this synthesis a *new* style. . . .

The stylistic intention of the mature work of Brunelleschi, strongly occupied with the actual "antique," becomes a decisive factor in the entire development of the new architecture.

With the adoption of the mass structure, he creates the basis of a "plastic architectural design": this is witnessed most impressively by the numerous drawings of the central building of the Angeli, and the further development of its scheme through the studies of Leonardo and Bramante to Michelangelo, who—especially in his sketches for S. Giovanni de' Fiorentini—exhausts the last possibilities of spatial plasticity. But the basis of Brunelleschi's creation reveals itself in the extent to which he absorbs the influence of the antique, and creates a new style in its fusion with tradition: he never was, and never wished to be, a copyist of antique architecture. Two years before Brunelleschi's death Michelozzo created the design for the choir of the SS. Annunziata in Florence after the pattern of the Minerva Medica in Rome. Brunelleschi's criticism of this first copy after the antique, which has been preserved, is characteristic enough: the sharp rejection, "because the 'convenienza' of the church is not considered, and the building is, in addition, completely inadequate for its purposes," [15] shows the conscious way in which he absorbed the antique in his creation without, however, striving to return to it. Alberti took over the completion of Michelozzo's project—despite violent attacks—and in his retention of this plan gives his recognition to Michelozzo's "canonic" style interpretation. Thus the lack of connection between Brunelleschi and Alberti, which Geymüller finds so inexplicable, has a profound basis: the theoretician, Alberti, could find few points of contact for his classic stylistic intention in the works of Brunelleschi, however great his veneration for "the founder of the new architecture." . . .

The *synthetic* thinking of Brunelleschi, which allows his own style to form itself in an interplay with the "historical," and to manifest itself in free and independent reworking and transformation—it is this synthetic thinking which indicates the direction for the further development of the new style. It stands in a different—freer—relation to the antique than the "canonic" one of Michelozzo and Alberti. The fact that Sangallo and especially Leonardo—the founders of a stylistic tendency which leads beyond the "classic style" to an "unclassical trend" of the High Renaissance—are connected not with Alberti but rather with the late Brunelleschi, allows us to understand not only the whole productivity of the first solution of the style problem of the Renaissance in Brunelleschi's work, but also to recognize his "individual style" from a different viewpoint: in the progress of the "historical(ly determined) style of the Renaissance" (Burckhardt), the problem of individual style

[15] Cf. Braghiralli, *Repertorium für Kunstwissenschaft*, II (1879), 272 (Doc. XI), and *Mitteilungen des Kunsthistorischen Instituts in Florenz* (1930), H. 5.

is based on the continually renewed, always changing, characteristic interplay of the artistic personality with antique and recent heritage, in the resultant definition of his requirements. In the connection between the new style and the personality, however, consists also his inner independence, which permits him to develop beyond the simply "derivative" to an "organic style" in Burckhardt's sense of the word.

Howard Saalman
From *Filippo Brunelleschi:*
Capital Studies (1958)

In recent literature the term capital studies has become identified to some degree with mediaeval studies. Gütschow,[1] Weigand [2] and others[3] have studied antique capitals. Kautsch's work on late antique and early Christian capitals,[4] though not more than a preliminary survey, remains as unique as it is indispensable. But it is in the study of Romanesque and Gothic buildings that systematic, analytical, and comparative capital studies have been most widely applied and with considerable success. Historians of architecture since the nineteenth century[5] have ex-

---

Reprinted from H. Saalman "Filippo Brunelleschi: Capital Studies," in *The Art Bulletin*, 40 (1958), 113–16, by permission of the author. Illustrations from the original article have not been reproduced.

[1] M. Gütschow, "Untersuchungen zum korinthischen Kapitell," *Jbh. d. deutschen archäol. Inst.*, XXXVI, 1921, pp. 44–83.
[2] E. Weigand, "Baalbek und Rom, die römische Reichskunst in ihrer Entwicklung und Differenzierung," *Jbh. d. K.-deutschen archäol. Inst.*, XXIX, 1914, pp. 37–91.
[3] H. Kähler, *Die römischen Kapitelle des Rheingebiets* (Römisch-germanische Forschungen, 13), Berlin, 1939; and many others.
[4] R. Kautsch, *Kapitellstudien*, Berlin, 1936.
[5] G. Dehio and G. v. Bezold, *Die kirchliche Baukunst des Abendlandes,* Stuttgart, 1892–1901, I, pp. 667f.

amined the capitals of mediaeval buildings as keys to style, regional
groupings and reciprocal influences, identification of local workshops
and the definition of progressive building periods in single monuments.
Such studies have proven singularly fruitful and have led to clarifica-
tion of many basic problems.

Two factors have combined to make capital studies an important
tool for the historian of mediaeval architecture: the relatively large
number of surviving monuments, permitting the observation of a fairly
clear and continuous development of architectural forms, and the
scarcity of documented historical data. Thus the reliably dated architectural details of just one building have served, in some instances, as
the basis for the chronological definition of a whole group of related
but entirely undocumented monuments.[6]

Comprehensive and systematic studies of Early Renaissance
Florentine architectural details, however, have been begun only recently. The reasons are obvious. The relative increase of documentary
data in fourteenth, fifteenth, and sixteenth century Italy, the appearance of identifiable artists, architects, and patrons whose activities
and whereabouts can be traced, dated, and followed, have tended to
focus the attention of historians, not improperly, on the wealth of data
to be extracted from the archives, histories, biographies and other written sources which become ever more numerous at this time. The profu-
sion of surviving and often signed and dated, or, at least, readily
datable panels, altarpieces, and frescoes in or from Trecento and
Quattrocento buildings provide quantities of important data useful for
defining the development of various buildings. Nevertheless, the fact
remains that painful gaps in the knowledge of Early Renaissance architecture are the rule rather than the exception. Thus, the utilization of
the tried and proven technique of systematic and comparative capital
studies as an additional means of research seems overdue. The results
of a comprehensive examination of Brunelleschian capitals presented
here are, therefore, offered both for the light they shed on a number of
previously unsolved problems concerning this most important of Early
Renaissance architects and as the fruits of a pilot study in an almost

---

[6] See, e.g., W. Horn, "Das florentiner Baptisterium," *Mitt. d. Kunsthist. Inst. in
Florenz*, v, 1938, pp. 100–151; *idem*, "Romanesque Churches in Florence, A
Study of Their Chronology and Stylistic Development," *Art Bulletin*, xxv,
1943, pp. 112f.; and many others.

uncharted field.[7] It is in the nature of capital studies that one looks at the trees rather than the forest. Yet, emerging from the mass of detail, the total scene can be viewed with deeper insight and greater conviction.

I

In considering the nature of the architectural vocabulary of the first half of the fifteenth century, the comments of the writers of the later fifteenth and sixteenth centuries furnish an unreliable criterion. Beginning with the anonymous author of the Brunelleschi *Vita* in the late 1480's and continuing with Vasari and later writers, it is stated and restated that Brunelleschi brought back the good architecture of the ancients with particular emphasis on the Vitruvian orders.[8] This characterization must be evaluated in relation to the period in which it was made. By the early 1480's Alberti's *De re aedificatoria* had received wide circulation and the Anonymous refers to it directly and indirectly. It has not been sufficiently emphasized just how much of the Brunelleschi *Vita* is based on Alberti's treatise. While Alberti's ideas may have received impetus from his association with Brunelleschi and may be founded in part on Brunelleschi's work, it can nevertheless be suggested that much of the archaeological activity the Anonymous ascribes to his hero is based on the example of Alberti. In the early 1480's the respectable architectural hero simply *had* to concern himself with perspective experiments, excavate among Roman ruins and make drawings of ancient capitals, cornices, etc.[9] The absorption of a vocabu-

---

[7] Dr. Martin Gosebruch, Hamburg, has kindly allowed me to peruse the manuscript of his article on sources and development of early Renaissance capitals, which will appear in one of the future volumes of *Römisches Jbh. für Kunstgeschichte* [VIII (1958), 65ff.—Ed.]. Covering a wider field, Dr. Gosebruch often comes to similar conclusions in his discussion of Brunelleschi capitals.

[8] A. Manetti, *Vita di Brunellesco*, ed. Toesca, Florence, 1927. For a discussion of various problems connected with the *vita* and its authorship, cf. J. Schlosser, *La letteratura artistica*, ed. O. Kurz, Florence, 1956, pp. 119–120. See also, Peter Murray, "Art Historians and Art Critics—IV, XIV Uomini Singhularii in Firenze," *Burlington Magazine*, xcix, 1957, pp. 330f.

[9] I will discuss the Brunelleschi *vita* in further studies on Brunelleschi in preparation. [Since published: *The Life of Brunelleschi by Antonio di Tuccio Manetti*, Introduction, Notes and Critical Text Edition by H. Saalman, transl. by C. Enggass, University Park and London, 1970.—Ed.]

lary *all'antico* by the Early Renaissance architects can also not be made dependent on the dates and frequency of their trips to Rome because they grew up in an environment abounding with Romanesque buildings constructed in part with Roman spoils, preserving a definite antique flavor and considered at the time and for some centuries thereafter to be at least partly antique monuments. The antique forms had never died out in Florence after the eleventh and twelfth century Protorenaissance and continued to characterize the architecture of the Gothic centuries.

Already in the later nineteenth century Dehio saw the major source of Brunelleschian architecture in the Tuscan Protorenaissance.[10] Since then this connection has, perhaps, been somewhat overemphasized. For the very reason that Brunelleschian capitals in particular bear little resemblance to genuine antique capitals, they also differ considerably from Florentine Protorenaissance capitals which were careful imitations after antique models, so careful that the fine eye of a specialist is required to distinguish the Romanesque imitations from the original spoils.[11] It is, in fact, surprising—in view of the multiplicity of spoils to be seen everywhere in Florence and elsewhere in the Toscana—how different from any antique prototype Brunelleschi's capitals actually are, compared with the not uncommon classicizing Corinthian capitals of Dugento and Trecento masons.

It is, however, the essential peculiarity and characteristic of Brunelleschian capitals from the beginning, and thus relevant to Brunelleschi's entire architectural method and style, that their elements were derived largely from the immediate Tuscan surroundings and combined in greatly simplified and reduced form. Only in Brunelleschi's latest period can the influence of genuine antique prototypes be clearly demonstrated. This passion for reduction and regularization of forms and the absolute uniformity of identical details comprise the novelty and distinguishing characteristic of Brunelleschi's style and, to an extent, that of his contemporaries in the second and third decades of the fifteenth century. This, and not the "revival" of antique forms, marks the new capitals of the Early Renaissance artists.

I will discuss some of the specific Brunelleschi sources in connec-

---

[10] G. Dehio, "Romanische Renaissance," *Jbh. d. k.-preuss. Kunstsamml.*, VII, 1886, p. 129.

[11] W. Horn, *op. cit.*, pp. 145–147.

tion with the individual monuments. However, at this point we might compare Brunelleschi's tendency to reduce the parts of his capitals to a minimum with similar tendencies in a group of Tuscan Romanesque capitals less classicizing than those of the Protorenaissance group. The leaf type of his early Innocenti capitals is the basis for comparison. The leaf surface is a flat mass, rolled out like cake batter. The surrounding mass is cut out cleanly against the *calathos* [capital core—Ed.]. The leaf tips are usually three rounded-off tongues at the upper end of the rib incisions. At the upper crest the leaf becomes suddenly pasty and thick. The crest falls forward in a massive fan divided into a main center tongue with a smaller tongue on each side.

This particular leaf type is characteristically Tuscan and can be traced back to the late twelfth and early thirteenth centuries. A late Romanesque example appears on one of the nave capitals in the Cathedral of Fiesole (ca. 1201). Its leaves are very similar to the Innocenti type in outline and internal detail. The *caules* [stalks—Ed.] are identical smooth round stalks with a ring of little pointed leaves at the crest. Then, however, follow antiquizing *folia projecta* [projecting leaves—Ed.], very flat long *helices* [inner volutes—Ed.] and a sculptured head in place of the abacus blossom.

The connection of the Innocenti capitals with this capital in Fiesole is of particular interest. Biehl has identified it and others in this church as rather late examples of a Tuscan provincial sculptural style which developed around the middle of the twelfth century under primary Lombard and secondary French influences.[12] Examples of this type are found in the area of Arezzo, the Casentino, and the upper Arno valley. This style is distinguished from the prevailing upper Italian art through broader, fleshier, quieter forms. Other types where twelfth century French influences are more pronounced also find rather more primitive expression at the hands of the Tuscan provincial masons. Such capitals, e.g., portal capitals from the Badia Sant'Antimo (ca. 1140) in Castelnuovo dell'Abate near Siena may be seen in relation to Brunelleschi's tendency to reduce his elements to their simplest forms, giving the background to such Brunelleschian phenomena as the merged volutes that characterize Brunelleschi's Innocenti and San Lorenzo capitals, the *caules* reduced to slight swellings on the *calathos*

---

[12] W. Biehl, *Toskanische Plastik des frühen und hohen Mittelalters*, Leipzig, 1926, pp. 28 and 103, n. 37 to ch. 2; pls. 3f.

surface in his Barbadori, San Lorenzo, and Pazzi capitals and the absence of developed *folia projecta.*

The local sculptural tradition is, in itself, of only limited interest. However, it contains forms congenial to Brunelleschi's primary aesthetic intention.

Striking illustrations of stylistic consistency between larger design and detail ornament, Brunelleschi's capitals reflect his total architectural conception during every stage of his development. During the Innocenti period Brunelleschi's capital vocabulary, rooted in the Tuscan Gothic tradition of stone masonry, had perhaps not quite caught up with the radical regularity of the ground plan and elevation of the *Spedale,* though this too had its precursors in the late fourteenth and early fifteenth centuries.[13]

The rectangular and square spatial organization which marks Brunelleschi's San Lorenzo period is mirrored in the linear composition and flat relief and in the rather hard leaf and volute style of the 1420's. The eleventh and twelfth century Tuscan Romanesque architecture which contributed elements to the earlier capitals is now the primary source. This is particularly noticeable in Brunelleschi's new conception of the acanthus leaf as a flat semi-elliptical solid, vertically striated by nearly parallel incised ribs which curve out lightly near the top. Only around the leaf fringes of the San Lorenzo capitals are concessions made to sculptural modification. On the leaf surface itself little sickle-shaped incisions are the sole modeling. The decorative principle of the leaf as a flat incised solid is closely related to that of Tuscan Romanesque capitals where this type in variations is almost the rule. A few typical examples among the abundance of related types may be mentioned, e.g., various capitals in San Giovanni and S. Apostoli, Florence, and the Pisan Baptistery.[14]

In his late phase Brunelleschi conceived of buildings as mass to be molded and hollowed out, divided by plastic half-columns instead of flat pilasters, maintaining essentially simple plain surface and restrained plastic ornamentation. All these late characteristics are reflected in Brunelleschi's late capitals at the Cappella Pazzi. The capital

---

[13] G. Marchini, "La chiesa di San Agostino in Prato e l'architettura fiorentina tardo gotica," *Rivista d'Arte,* xx, 1938, pp. 105–122.

[14] [M. Salmi, *L'architettura romanica in Toscana* (Milan and Rome, 1927), pl. 240.]

is more organic, more "antique." The subtle means of connecting parts organically find their prototype in genuine antique capitals of the middle Imperial Roman period. Both the so-called "spoon leaf" type of the Pazzi capitals[15] as well as the fine incision on the center of each leaf by means of which the center *folium* of the upper row is connected organically to the lower, appear on a capital of perhaps the late first century in San Miniato and on antique capitals in San Giovanni and elsewhere. The earlier linear conception has given way to more plastic treatment. The pilaster *calathos* curves outward, the volutes and other members are handled more softly. But there is no increase in complexity of the parts. The typically antique *caules* and *folia projecta* are not adopted.

[15] M. Meurer, *Vergleichende Formenlehre des Ornaments und der Pflanze*, Dresden, 1909, pp. 140f.

Richard Krautheimer
Brunelleschi and Linear
Perspective, in *Lorenzo Ghiberti*
(1956)

A correct linear perspective construction, that is, a mathematically controllable one, had been worked out among Florentine artists ten or fifteen years before Ghiberti designed the panels of his second door. It is generally agreed that Filippo Brunelleschi was the key figure in its achievement. Why otherwise should Alberti have dedicated his *Treatise*

Selections from Chapter XVI, "Linear Perspective" (with cuts) in Richard Krautheimer and Trude Krautheimer-Hess, *Lorenzo Ghiberti*, Reissue (copyright © 1970 by Princeton University Press), Vol. I, pp. 234–45. Reprinted by permission of Princeton University Press. Bibliography cited in footnotes appears immediately following this selection.

on Painting in 1435 to him, an architect, unless that architect had made an essential contribution to painting—more specifically a contribution to the very problem of perspective with which the first book of Alberti's treatise is exclusively concerned? Indeed, in or about 1463 Filarete mentioned Brunelleschi specifically as the discoverer of perspective and around 1480 the master's first biographer set forth the invention of perspective as one of the major achievements of his hero's early years, before 1420. This assertion is confirmed by Manetti's *Uomini singholari*.[1] Vasari, in his first edition of 1550 promulgates the tradition as common knowledge.

According to the *Vita di Brunellesco,* the ancients, though possibly they knew the practice, did not know the theory of perspective, and for that reason Brunelleschi had to invent practice and theory anew. The biographer had seen with his own eyes two of Brunelleschi's experimental perspective paintings, both on wood. One represented the Piazza de'Signori with its surrounding buildings, among them the Palazzo Vecchio, whose north and west façades were clearly shown. The sky of the panels was sawed out, so that if the painting were placed at a clearly defined point some *braccia* towards Or San Michele and the spectator stood at another fixed point some *braccia* distant, the skyline of the painting would coincide exactly with that of the real buildings. The second panel was about half a *braccio* square and represented a view of the piazza in front of the Cathedral, drawn from a point "three *braccia* or so" inside the main portal. It showed "that part of the piazza which the eye can see," including the Baptistery and part of the buildings bordering the square. The sky in this painting, rather than being cut out, was covered with burnished reflecting silver. Now, so the biographer goes on, "the painter must assume one single point from which his painting should be seen in relation to both the upper and lower limits and the lateral boundaries (si per altezza e bassezza e da' lati) of the picture, as well as the distance (come per discosto)." Thus, "to prevent the spectator from falling into error" by choosing a wrong point of view, Brunelleschi had drilled through the panel a hole "which fell in the painting in the direction of the temple of San Giovanni at the point where the eye struck, opposite a beholder looking out from inside the center door of Santa Maria del Fiore where

[1] Alberti, bibl. 8, pp. 47ff; Filarete, bibl. 158, pp. 609, 619, 621; (Manetti), bibl. 294, pp. 9ff; Manetti, bibl. 293, p. 163.

he would have taken his position had he painted it" (che veniva a essere nel dipinto della parte del tempio di San Giovanni in quello luogo dove percoteva l'occhio al diritto da chi guardava da quello luogo dentro alla porta del mezzo di Santa Maria del Fiore dove si sarebbe posto se l'avesse ritratto). "This hole was small as a lentil on the painted side," while "on the back of the panel it opened out in pyramidal [i.e. conical] form to the size of a ducat or a little more like the crown of a woman's straw hat." Then with one hand the spectator should hold the back of the painting against his eye and look through the larger end of the hole at a flat mirror held in the other hand at arm's length. The painting would thus be reflected in the mirror; and this extension (*dilazione*)[2] of the hand with the mirror would correspond to the approximate distance [from the Baptistery] in *braccia piccoline*. The reflection of the sky and the moving clouds in the silver-coated upper part of the painting would heighten the impression of reality.

The basic principles involved in Brunelleschi's perspective construction were for the first time elucidated by Panofsky many years ago.[3] The following is merely an attempt to trace Brunelleschi's perspective procedure step by step in the light of the specific topographical conditions within which he worked. He placed himself inside the Cathedral, three odd *braccia* behind the main portal. Thus he stood exactly 60 *braccia* from the Baptistery.[4] The floor level of the Cathedral rose about one *braccio* above the piazza, and given Brunelleschi's diminutive height, to which his biographer attests, his eye would have been 3 to 3½ *braccia* above the piazza. The portal of the

[2] The *Accademia della Crusca* (bibl. 1, IV, p. 326) renders *dilatare* as "accrescere in distanza o distenzione," (increase in distance or extension).

[3] Panofsky, bibl. 385, particularly pp. 258f, 283, and a lucid summary *in nuce* bibl. 379, pp. 91ff, particularly pp. 93–96; see also Bunim, bibl. 81, pp. 186ff, White, bibl. 552, Wittkower, bibl. 558, and recently Siebenhüner and others, in a discussion, reported in *Kunstchronik* 1954, pp. 129f.

[4] The following measurements were obtained in a survey of the site in 1951. The distance from the Gates of Paradise to the inner boundary of the threshold on the main gate of the Cathedral amounts to 32.80 m. By adding three and one third *braccia*, 2.04 m, one arrives at 34.84 m, just 20 cm short of 60 *braccia*. Within this total, 7.82 m correspond to the distance from Brunelleschi's position inside the Cathedral to the far edge of the platform in front of the church, an additional 1.74 m to the width of the stairs ascending to the platform. The level of the platform above the present level of the square, 0.75 m must be discounted. The original difference in level, according to the excellent survey of Sgrilli (bibl. 491, pls. I, II, IV) appears to have been only 0.60 m.

church framed his field of vision both vertically and horizontally. At its upper boundary it would have been practically unlimited, the architrave being 13 *braccia* from the threshold; but at the bottom it would have been cut off by the platform in front of the door and by the four steps ascending from the square. The edge of this platform, 13½ *braccia* from his position, was bound to eliminate from Brunelleschi's field of vision roughly 20 *braccia* of the piazza, one third of the total distance to the Baptistery. The limitations of the horizontal angle of vision were even more severe; for given the width of the door, only 6½ *braccia*, he could see, beyond the looming mass of the Baptistery, only a small section on either side at the far ends of the piazza. At the point where his eye would hit the piazza first, beyond the edge of the platform and 20 *braccia* from where he stood, the section he could see was exactly 30 *braccia* wide.[5]

These data of the topographical situation were supplemented by Brunelleschi's use of a mirror, or rather of two mirrors: for since the picture was to be viewed in a mirror held by the outstretched hand it must have been a mirrorlike left to right reversal of the original. Therefore, it was either painted on a mirror (hence the silvercoated reflecting surface) or with the help of a mirror placed alongside the panel.

The use of a mirror in verifying the phenomena of linear perspective was common Quattrocento practice. Indeed, three-dimensional relationships in a mirror are automatically transferred onto a two-dimensional surface as they would be in a drawing by means of a perspective construction. Filarete probably codified an old tradition when stating that the mirror revealed perspective elements which could not be seen with the naked eye: the squares of a floor or the beams of a ceiling appear to converge in the distance, "and if you want to see this more

---

[5] Mr. John White has been good enough to make accessible to me the manuscript of his dissertation, University of London, 1952. In discussing Brunelleschi's perspective, Mr. White points out that Brunelleschi's field of vision was further limited by the porch which then projected in front of the portal of the Cathedral as seen in the drawing of the façade of 1587 (Poggi, bibl. 413, p. xxiii). Therefore, Mr. White thinks of Brunelleschi's position as three *braccia* inside the porch and barely beyond the sill of the door, so as to allow him to see more of the piazza. But it seems significant indeed that Brunelleschi's biographer places such stress on the far corners of the piazza, the *Canto alla Paglia* and the *Canto de'Pecori*, being represented. Thus, one wonders whether the greater part of the sides of the piazza was not really cut off.

clearly, take a mirror and look into it. And you will clearly see this to be so. But if the same were opposite your naked eye, they would seem but equidistant to you." He adds that in his opinion it was through the use of a mirror that "Pippo di Ser Brunellesco from Florence found the procedure to evolve this method (of perspective) which indeed was a subtle and beautiful thing, that he discovered by reasoning what you see in the mirror." [6] While this statement obviously need not be taken literally, it is at least possible that Brunelleschi originally designed the view of the Piazza del Duomo on the reflecting surface of burnished silver as a means of control for his perspective construction.

Still, the important mirror was not the one on which or with the aid of which Brunelleschi painted, but the one in which the painting was reflected; for it served to fix the exact point from which the painting was to be viewed. By drilling a hole through the panel and making the spectator peep through it at the reflection in the mirror, and by leaving the sky of the painting a reflecting surface which would register any difference between the skyline of the original objects and that of the painting. Brunelleschi forced him to occupy the exact point from which he himself had viewed the piazza and to look at exactly the point on the Baptistery façade at which he himself had looked as well as to hold the mirror at a specific distance from the painting. Thus Brunelleschi made two sets of points coincide: that from which he had seen the object and the point opposite on the façade of the Baptistery, and the "view point" of the spectator and the corresponding point of the Baptistery in the painting.

All this makes sense only on the assumption that Brunelleschi started out from the concept of a constant mathematical and proportional relation between the reality of the object and its representation. His biographer leaves no doubt in this respect, saying, it may be recalled, that the "extension" of the beholder's outstretched arm between panel and mirror corresponded to the distance from the Baptistery *a braccia piccoline*. Within his vocabulary this term always signifies a

---

[6] Filarete, bibl. 158, pp. 608f. See also Alberti, bibl. 8, p. 135: "Objects taken from nature should be corrected with the mirror . . . ; for objects well painted, I do not know how, have much gracefulness in a mirror, and it is wonderful how each defect of a painting shows distorted in the mirror." The Latin version (bibl. 10, p. 14) differs slightly in wording.

relation in scale,[7] and a definite relation in scale was indeed the key-
stone in Brunelleschi's perspective procedure.

It was easy to calculate such a relation for the Piazza del Duomo
panel. The distance from the painting to its mirror reflection being one
braccio, and that from the eye to the Baptistery, 60 *braccia*, the scale
was 1:60, a normal ratio in any duodecimal system. Brunelleschi had
evidently chosen his standpoint very carefully so as to arrive at this
particular proportion. The line that marked what was for him the
piazza's near boundary, was 30 *braccia* long, exactly half the distance
from his eye to the Baptistery; thus it corresponded in scale to the
width of the panel, which was one half *braccio*. In other words, Brunelleschi established in scale both distance and base line of his painting.
Since the panel was square, the proportions of distance to width to
height were 2:1:1.

If, then, Brunelleschi drew to scale *a braccia piccoline* both the
distance from the Cathedral to the Baptistery, and the base line of his
painting, he must have started out by making a ground plan of the entire square on a scale of 1:60, including in it his own position inside the
Cathedral. Plans and elevations drawn to scale in the early fifteenth
century were fundamental innovations of architectural tooling, and if
Brunelleschi's biographer is correct, Brunelleschi was the first to intro-
duce them in Florence. On this plan of the piazza he must have marked
the horizontal visual angle as determined by the portal jambs through
which he gazed. The location of all points on this horizontal plane,
such as the corners of the Baptistery and piazza, were indicated in the
ground plan by lines extending from his position. On the same scale as
the plan, he would draw elevations: one of the Baptistery and the
buildings behind, and two at right angles to this, each including his
position, the Baptistery and the right and left sides of the piazza respectively. Since the Baptistery appeared the same from all three sides, the
three elevations were practically interchangeable. By means of these
elevations, the location of all points within the vertical angle of vision

---

[7] (Manetti), bibl. 294, with reference to the drawing for the Innocenti portico,
p. 56 and to the model for S. Spirito. Mr. Wolfgang Lotz has been good enough
to call my attention to a passage quoted by Oertel (bibl. 367, p. 261 with older
bibliography), expressly stating that as early as 1390 the model of S. Petronio
in Bologna was made to scale.

could be marked out again by lines connecting them with his eye point.

Within such a construction, achieved by means of a plan and elevations, it was desirable for purposes of location to indicate the greatest possible number of points, which would form a network over all the structures to be represented. Indeed, Brunelleschi's biographer states that to survey ancient buildings in Rome the master used parchment strips and transferred the measurement to paper ". . . marked by numbers and letters"; in brief, to graph paper with the coordinates marked both vertically and horizontally, a system "which Filipo by himself understood," that is, a method of his own invention. The Baptistery, with its geometric marble incrustation could easily be adapted to such a system of coordinates and hence would have made an ideal testing ground for Brunelleschi's method of perspective construction.[8]

After locating the greatest possible number of points on both plan and elevation, the next step was simple: Brunelleschi must have drawn a transverse line across the ground plan at the exact point where his eye first hit the piazza at the lower limit of his vertical angle of vision. The points of intersection on this transversal marked by lines drawn within the horizontal angle of vision from his position to the key points of the Baptistery and piazza were then transferred to the base line of the panel. In an analogous operation he dropped a perpendicular through the elevations at a point corresponding to the transversal on the ground plan. The intersections of this perpendicular with the vertical sight lines that Brunelleschi had drawn from his position to key points on the Baptistery and background buildings he then transferred to the right and left edges of the panel. Finally, beginning from these marked points along the base and sides, he could draw a network of

[8] (Manetti), bibl. 294, p. 21. Brunelleschi and Donatello, in surveying the heights of ancient buildings ". . . dove e' potevano congetturare l' altezza . . . ponevano in su striscie di pergamene che si lievano per riquadrare le carte con numero d'abaco e caratte[re], che Filipo intendeva per se medesimo" (The comma between *carte* and *con* can be omitted). Prager (bibl. 425, in particular, pp. 539f; see also Lowry, bibl. 280) has correctly suggested such scale drawings of plans and elevations as the basic element of Brunelleschi's perspective construction. He has also stressed the likelihood of Brunelleschi's having used graph paper as a tool for establishing the vertical and horizontal coordinates on both his scale and perspective drawings.

vertical and horizontal lines on the panel, their intersections establishing the exact location of each point of the buildings. Whatever their angle to the picture plane, parallel, orthogonal, or oblique, all lines of the perspective picture of the object could easily be drawn by simply connecting on the panel the corresponding points of intersection. Combining the horizontal and vertical visual angles, through which in a number of independent drawings he had linked his "eye-point" to the largest possible number of points on the object, he coordinated them eventually into a final perspective design. The result was a perspective picture arrived at by what later theorists called the *costruzione legittima* (Diagram).[9] Alberti's *intersegazione* appears to be nothing but the physical reproduction of this linear network by a "veil" of strings, and, indeed, Vasari contended that Brunelleschi drew his perspective by way of ground plan, elevation, and *intersegazione*.

However, to Brunelleschi the *eye point* in the picture was not necessarily what we know as a *vanishing point*. Its position on the picture plane was not arbitrarily assumed so as to serve as the starting point for the orthogonals. On the contrary, if we interpret Brunelleschi's biographer correctly, in his construction this point served only to fix the position of the spectator's eye in relation to both painting and reality and the distance from which the painting should be viewed. It was, therefore, a coordinator to begin with—a stable pole of reference for the position of artist, object, spectator, and representation. The orthogonals converged towards it, as a result of Brunelleschi's construction, but not because it was the vanishing point from the outset. Likewise, this point would seem not to have been located in the center of the panel. On the contrary, it must have been far down, roughly 8 cm from the picture base, corresponding exactly to the level at which Brunelleschi's horizontal sight line struck the façade of the Baptistery.

Brunelleschi, then, proceeded along lines strictly architectural in thought. His aim was architectural and practical: one suspects that he worked out his procedure as a means of representing building projects in perspective and to scale, and of surveying existing architecture, whether Roman ruins or architectural sites in Florence. His methods of architectural representation were those of a practicing architect; that

[9] Panofsky, bibl. 385, p. 283; bibl. 379, p. 93. Since Brunelleschi's picture of Piazza del Duomo showed three sides of the square, its construction must have required three rather than just one elevation.

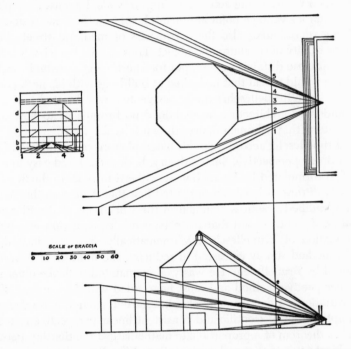

DIAGRAM. Brunelleschi, Perspective Construction, Piazza del Duomo

is, he worked only with ground plans and elevations drawn to scale on a mathematical basis.

Brunelleschi's perspective method was fundamentally an architectural tool. True, it could be used for pictorial ends by drawing plan and elevation of one or more imaginary buildings. Indeed, a consensus of opinions towards the end of the century held that the practice of linear perspective in both painting and sculpture derived directly from Brunelleschi's construction.[10] But as first evolved by Brunelleschi, the method could hardly become a popular tool for painters. It was un-

[10] (Manetti), bibl. 294, p. 163.

wieldy, requiring a number of preliminary drawings followed by complicated transferral of coordinate points to the final panel. It was apt to result in rapid foreshortenings. Since Brunelleschi's principal preoccupation was drawing actual buildings to *scale,* he must have placed the spectator's vantage point at a man's height on the same scale as the building represented; also the narrowness of medieval streets forced close proximity of spectator and object. Thus, both a low viewpoint and a view at close distance made rapid foreshortenings inevitable and the drawing would reveal that he looked at buildings with his neck craned. Finally, since Brunelleschi's linear perspective was devoted to the representation of architecture, it contained no formula as to how to incorporate within it human figures drawn to scale. . . .

Brunelleschi, according to his biographer, never formulated a theory of linear perspective. Such a theory, both correct and easy to apply was first formulated by Leone Battista Alberti in 1435, in the first book of *Della Pittura.* It has been suggested first that Alberti in this treatise merely codified practices common in the workshops of the Florentine *avant-garde,* and second that his perspective construction was but an abbreviation of Brunelleschi's. Mathematically speaking, indeed, Alberti's method simply consisted in reducing the number of operations required by Brunelleschi. He was well acquainted with the older master's perspective method and must have sided with him against shortcut variations. Like Brunelleschi, he started from the fundamental assumption that a scientific and consistent linear perspective rested on Euclid's theorem of a proportionate mathematical relationship between the object and its pictorial presentation. Like Brunelleschi, he established for the artist a position fixed in height and distance from both object and painting, and thus identical for both painter and beholder. But what counted for his contemporaries was the practice, and with all due respect for Brunelleschi, young Alberti in his treatise left little doubt regarding the distinctiveness and the advantages of his own method. Indeed, his approach differs from Brunelleschi's on three counts: his procedure was methodically founded on theory: his method was simpler and better adjusted to a painters' needs; his aim was to present a measurable space for the action of figures, not to represent buildings as an architect.

BIBLIOGRAPHY

1. Accademia della Crusca, *Vocabulario della lingua italiana*, 5th ed., Florence, 1863ff.

8. L. B. ALBERTI, *Leone Battista Alberti's Kleinere Kunsttheoretische Schriften* (*Della Pittura libri tre; De statua; I cinque ordini Architettonici*), ed. H. Janitschek (*Quellenschriften für Kunstgeschichte*, ed. R. Eitelberger von Edelberg, XI), Vienna, 1877.

10. L. B. ALBERTI, *De Pictura*, in: M. Vitruvius Pollio, *De Architectura*, Amsterdam, 1649, pp. 165ff.

81. M. SCHILD BUNIM, *Space in Mediaeval Painting and the Forerunners of Perspective*, New York, 1940.

158. ANTONIO AVERLINO FILARETE, *Tractat über die Baukunst . . .* , ed. W. von Oettingen (*Quellenschriften für Kunstgeschichte, N. F.,* III), Vienna, 1896.

280. B. LOWRY, "Letter to the Editor." *Art Bulletin,* XXXV (1953), pp. 175ff.

293. ANTONIO MANETTI, *Uomini singholari*, in: *Operette istoriche*, ed. G. Milanesi, Florence, 1887.

294. (ANTONIO MANETTI), *Vita di Filippo Brunelleschi*, ed. E. Toesca, Rome, 1927.

367. R. OERTEL, "Wandmalerei und Zeichnung in Italien," *Mitteilungen des Kunsthistorischen Instituts in Florenz,* V (1937–40), pp. 217ff.

379. E. PANOFSKY, *The Codex Huygens and Leonardo da Vinci's Art Theory*, (*Studies of the Warburg Institute*, 13), London, 1940.

385. E. PANOFSKY, "Die Perspektive als symbolische Form," *Vorträge der Bibliothek Warburg*, 1924–25, Leipzig and Berlin, 1927, pp. 258ff.

413. G. POGGI, *Il Duomo di Firenze* (*Kunsthistorisches Institut in Florenz, Italienische Forschungen*, II), Berlin, 1909.

425. F. D. PRAGER, "Brunelleschi's Inventions and the Renewal of Roman Masonry Work," *Osiris,* IX (1950), pp. 457ff.

491. B. S. SGRILLI, *Descrizione e studj della . . . fabrica di S. Maria del Fiore . . .* , Florence, 1733.

552. J. WHITE, "Developments in Renaissance Perspective," *Journal of the Warburg and Courtauld Institutes,* XII (1949), pp. 58ff; XIV (1951), pp. 42ff.

558. R. WITTKOWER, "Brunelleschi and 'Proportion in Perspective,'" *Journal of the Warburg and Courtauld Institutes,* XVI (1953), pp. 275ff.

Frank D. Prager and
Gustina Scaglia
From *Brunelleschi, Studies of His*
Technology and Inventions
(1970)

BRUNELLESCHI AS
STRUCTURAL ENGINEER

The sources of Brunelleschi's ideas must be found in a Scholastic-Humanist world dominated by the Romanesque-Gothic structure of Arnolfo, Neri, and Ghini.[1] Beyond this, little is known of Filippo's schooling, his early technical experience, and the engineers who influenced him.

It is conceivable that he had contact with men of science, as he belonged to the higher classes of Florence. According to Manetti he knew Paolo dal Pozzo Toscanelli, a mathematician. However, nothing specific is known about talks between these men or work that they shared. If they ever discussed any of Filippo's architectural problems, the mathematician could hardly assist the practitioner in anything greater than perhaps the exact computation of some weights of material. There was no tradition and in fact not even a beginning in

Reprinted from *Brunelleschi, Studies of His Technology and Inventions*, pp. 61–64, 107–9, 135–37, by Frank D. Prager and Gustina Scaglia by permission of the M.I.T. Press, Cambridge, Massachusetts. Copyright © 1970 The Massachusetts Institute of Technology. Illustrations from the original text have not been reproduced.

[1] [Arnolfo di Cambio, Neri di Fioravante, Giovanni di Lapo Ghini were responsible for the planning of Florence Cathedral and its Cupola from the late thirteenth century through the late fourteenth century—Ed.]

contemporary science whereby anybody could have solved a more difficult problem, for example, the permissible loading and required dimensions of a building element such as a column, a pier, a rib, or a cupola shell. All these were designed on the basis of the roughest estimates, traditionally based on enormous overdesigning. Nor does it appear that Filippo himself ever undertook a mathematical or analytic investigation. His biographers describe some details of his perspective studies; even here they do not mention any part of the mathematical analysis that they knew to be pertinent. Nor do they suggest any other scientific activity of Filippo, beyond his quoting Dante and the Scriptures, which they mention with naïve defensiveness. They are not even aware of experimental observations, for example, a study of the behavior of the wood chain. The only real echoes of a scientific-technical study come from the rare reports about talks with other masters.

Filippo had one such talk with Mariano Taccola in Siena, and Taccola recorded it in a note that we consider in another study in this book.[2] The report is totally devoid of mathematics, but may suggest an interest in experimentation to explore the secrets of mechanics, hydraulics, and pneumatics. From Taccola's note and the entire evidence, it does not appear that Filippo had an urge to formulate his scientific or technical findings, particularly in written or illustrated form—although he was able to produce pungent expressions, as is shown by his sonnets and specifications. We hear some remark, without detail, about drawings that he made; they seem to be lost.[3] He worked extensively by means of models and full-scale constructions and not in general by writings or drawings.

He had pupils and admirers who witnessed his performance. Some of them in turn left a secondary record of his teachings, which in due course found a wide audience. For example, the engines in Taccola's treatises that have unmistakable Brunelleschian features reappear in many notebooks and treatises of the later Quattrocento, and so do the treatises of Taccola's indirect follower, Francesco di Giorgio.

[2] [Reprinted here, see above, pp. 30ff.—Ed.]

[3] Full-scale drawings on sand are reported by G. B. Gelli (ed. G. Mancini, *Arch. stor. italiano*, 1896, pp. 32ff.), and such techniques were widely known (Briggs, *The Architect*, pp. 89, 128). About Filippo's Roman drawings on ruled paper or parchment and his perspective apparatus, see *Manetti* [ed. E. Toesca—Ed.], pp. 10f., 20f., 56f., 78f. Also p. 28, about the question of cross-sectional views in orthogonal projection.

The existence of this secondary, graphic record was overlooked in the first edition of this study, but since that time many versions of Quattrocento books and portfolios of drawings were found; a beginning has been made toward establishing their sequence and nature. The machine drawings will be discussed in a study that follows. We cannot try at this point to describe the detailed architectural contents of the notebooks. Nor can we explore their complex relationships with the Renaissance of architecture, and mainly with that of Vitruvius (who in our opinion was substantially unknown to Brunelleschi and Taccola). However, we draw attention to the existence of these architectural drawings. They are combined with the machine drawings. The drawings of Brunelleschi's own time were collected, copied, recopied, developed, confused, and improved, and the resulting knowledge was studied by later architects, until this knowledge became universal and elementary. The drawings now known, in addition to those of machines, include representations of construction methods, foundations, building tools, building elements, building layouts, and various assemblies of buildings.[4] Further studies of this record will be needed if it is to become clearer than it is today how Filippo's conceptions entered into his mind or arose in it, and how he used and developed them.

At the present point we can see with some assurance that he used and developed both Gothic and Classic principles. He was an innovator of forms that remained fundamentally Gothic, and he was just as remarkable in this respect as he was in his well-known action as renewer of Classic forms. He made distinctive although limited use of buttresses and even pinnacles (on his Lantern) but avoided the use of transverse tie rods as he developed a "masonry" strengthened by at least four reinforcements: ribs, stone rings, wood chain, and segmental arches. Here he proved himself a more original and a more successful innovator than his predecessors in the Trecento and early Quattrocento. Here he also was much more successful than later

---

[4] Similar collections occur in earlier and later works, including, for example, the book of Villard de Honnecourt, ca. 1250 (ed. H. B. Hahnloser, Vienna, 1935); *Bellifortis* by Konrad Kyeser, ca. 1400 (ed. G. Quarg, Düsseldorf, 1967); *De ingeneis* by Mariano Taccola, 1433 (edition Prager-Scaglia, in preparation [published 1972, Cambridge, Mass.—Ed.]); and the *Trattati* of Francesco di Giorgio and followers, ca. 1480–1550. Also see Frankl, *The Gothic*, p. 145, about an unpublished "Vienna Sketchbook."

architects, who undertook to continue the construction of the cathedral of Milan.

Unfortunately part of his work remained unfinished. His followers
did not complete his Cupola. They failed to build the Gallery intended
to harmonize with his Exedras; yet this Gallery would be needed to
give full and clear expression to his structure. Baccio tried to build it;
Michelangelo halted the attempt. No one actually built it. There is
evidence permitting at least partial mental reconstruction of Filippo's
plan for uniting the Cupola-Tambour with the Little Tribunes,[5] but
the evidence is not sufficiently known and analyzed to justify more
than these general suggestions at present.

In its body as well as its Gallery area, the Cupola is less than
perfect. It has four plainly visible although minor cracks, which extend through four of the eight sides and also through large parts of the
understructure. They have been carefully studied by experts, including
G. B. Nelli about 1695 and P. L. Nervi and others about 1934.[6] It
was found that insertion of new tie rings would be possible but that

---

[5] Filippo, as well as his Trecento predecessors, may have expected to surround
the foot of the Cupola with statues or perhaps with pinnacles similar to those
on his Lantern. He provided platforms, perhaps for statues, in the masonry itself, at the foot ends of the outer ribs or *creste*, in or directly above the Gallery
zone overlying the Tambour. At each of these ends, four chain rods with outer
ring-shaped ends extend from the masonry.

[6] *Cupola* [C. Guasti, Florence, 1857—Ed.], pp. 209f., and Doc. 340 (1561). The
cracks, oddly, are located in the sides overlying the piers, not in the sides overlying the large Gothic arches between the piers. As might be expected, each
crack extends between the corner areas reinforced by the *volticcinole* [small
vaults—Ed.]. The facts, determined by P. L. Nervi and others and ably presented in *Rilievi* [Opera di S. Maria del Fiore, *Rilievi e Studi Sulla Cupola del
Brunelleschi*, Florence, 1939—Ed.], may be interpreted as indicating that the building is settling somewhat more on its south side than at the north; that as a
result the main piers and overlying masonry layers undergo shearing strains and
that strong ties (perhaps in the Tambour) reinforce the sides overlying the
Gothic arches. It is possible that earthquakes contribute to the settlement of
the supports and the formation of the cracks, in a gradual way. Some five to
ten earthquakes of significant strength occurred in Florence, between 1430 and
1580; fewer and lesser disturbances followed, between 1580 and 1690 (M. Ba-
ratta, *I terremoti in Italia*, Turin, 1901, p. 743). It seems that during and after
the latter years the cracks were substantially enlarged, giving rise to consulta-
tions of Nelli, Nervi, and others, also in 1954 and later. A new analysis by R. J.
Mainstone is about to appear in the *Transactions of the Newcomen Society*, for
1971.

they were not needed by the conditions thus far noted. These conditions are under more or less constant review.

The forces active in a cupola are complex. Their distribution and magnitude were unknown to Roman, Romanesque, Gothic, and Renaissance builders. Galileo, two centuries after Filippo, began to raise fundamental questions about such forces, and the next few generations of pupils, including Nelli, considered various aspects of these questions. In this way they continued the attempts of the Trecento masters and of Filippo himself. Directly after Nelli's time, while observations and studies were still limited to the cupolas of Florence and Rome, came the breakthrough of structural analysis, and the first few of the fundamental laws, now recognized in this field, were formulated.

It has been usual to say that Vasari overestimated Filippo, but it is possible that he did not estimate him highly enough. To us Filippo the architect appears as one of the great developers of Gothic building, as the principal founder of the Renaissance, and also as an important forerunner of modern structural design and analysis.

BRUNELLESCHI AS INVENTOR
OF MACHINES

Brunelleschi intended his machinery for the Florentine Cupola and also for wider application. . . . He may have led Florentine mechanics in new directions, but the question remains: Did he invent machines of general significance?

Surely his machines, as shown in the record considered here, amounted to more than the stone hangers admired by Manetti and Vasari. When one of the machines, such as the load positioner, was erroneously attributed to Leonardo, there were prompt exclamations about superior use of machine elements, as we have noted. However, a machine does not become historically significant because it is built by Leonardo, a great painter, or by Filippo, a great architect. If a machine invented by Filippo was a path-breaking innovation, one may expect to encounter its progeny in subsequent work, even if the invention be forgotten by the more philosophically inclined writers of architectural treatises.

The fact is that Filippo's complex machinery system and even his individual machines do not appear in subsequent building practice but only in notebooks and copybooks. Builders such as Antonio San Gallo returned to simpler methods. During the Cinquecento, Domenico Fontana had great popular success with his "Removal of the Vatican Obelisk." [7] The methods and machines that he used were elementary in comparison with Filippo's work. Nor did other mechanics, in Fontana's time, adopt mechanical systems comparable with those employed by Brunelleschi. Individual drawings of Mariano and his follower Francesco reappear in the Theaters of Machines, composed by the followers of Francesco. [8] Their development and even their plain reproduction no doubt served useful purposes. However, no one is known to have used or developed a mechanical system as advanced as that of Filippo, until the advent of the Industrial Revolution and its mechanized factories.

As might be expected under these circumstances, Brunelleschian machines are unknown to a historian of science and invention who wrote in Brunelleschi's century. The machines were noted by a Florentine historian of technology in the eighteenth century, but hardly beyond such limited extent as the machines had been described by Vasari. [9] Even Vasari is disregarded by modern historians of architecture and technology. [10] Even when other mechanical works of Gothic and Renaissance times were rediscovered, the character and achievement of the Brunelleschian machines remained forgotten. [11] Since then there has been no scarcity of interest in machinery concepts of various

[7] D. Fontana, *Della trasportazione dell' obelisco vaticano*, Rome, 1590, *passim*, and C. Fontana, *Templum vaticanum* [Rome, 1694—Ed.], pp. 109–173. See reproductions in Strauch, *History of Civil Engineering* [Cambridge, Mass., 1964—Ed.], pp. 99f. Also see Wittkower, *La cupola* [*La cupola di San Pietro di Michelangelo*, Florence, 1964—Ed.], Pls. 32, 34, 37, 39a, 41.

[8] L. Reti, "Francesco di Giorgio Martini's Treatise . . . and its Plagiarists," *Technology and Culture*, IV, 1963, pp. 287–298.

[9] Polydorus Vergilius, *De rerum inventoribus*, Venice, 1499; Manni, *De florentinis inventis* [Ferrara, 1731—Ed.], pp. 79–83.

[10] T. Beck, *Beiträge zur Geschichtes des Maschinenbaues*, Berlin, 1899; A. Wolf, *A History of Science, Technology and Philosophy in the Sixteenth and Seventeenth Centuries*, London, 1935; C. Singer et al., *A History of Technology*, II, III, Oxford, 1956–1957; A. Burstall, *A History of Mechanical Engineering*, Cambridge, Mass., 1965.

[11] Near the end of the eighteenth century, G. B. Venturi rediscovered the technical work of both Taccola and Leonardo. *Essai sur les ouvrages physico-mathématiques de Léonard de Vinci*, Paris, 1797. The publication led to a flood of popularizations of Leonardo.

times, and there has always been enormous interest, for example, in Galileo's technology as well as his science.[12] Nevertheless, and in spite of Brunelleschi's incomparable fame, strangely the present studies are among the first attempts to review the master's technical work, including his machine work, in some depth.

It is conceivable that Filippo was too far ahead of his time and therefore unable to influence his time with regard to machines. However, his system of hoisting and positioning devices hardly was reinvented even in later times. The progress of machinery, in those times, came about by studies in scientific technology, such as the mathematical and experimental analysis of gear-tooth profiles, lubricated bearings, and load-bearing posts or beams. These searching studies of simple things, not the developments of more complex devices, brought the major advances of modern technology. The fate of the Brunelleschian machines is comparable to that of refinements in Gothic tracery, forgotten in times of classic revival. It would be futile to insist that these machines were important to mechanical developments of later times. Perhaps they may be said to share the position of Filippo's method of vaulting without armature. In striking contrast to Filippo's structural and stylistic innovations, these famous machines and methods would now appear as matters of local and temporary sensation, not of major historic significance.

We are stating this in an effort to avoid misinterpretations of the mechanical work. We do not consider Filippo's machines as important inventions in the progress of machinery, but we consider them as most interesting elements in Filippo's progress. Some of his powers and also some of his limitations are shown with unequaled clarity in the record set forth by Ghiberti, the Opera, Taccola, San Gallo, and Manetti. For this reason the record is in need of further study. There may be manuscripts thus far undiscovered, which may throw further light on the development of Brunelleschian machines and related matters. We hardly think that all of these have been found, and we are sure they have not been evaluated in a final way.

So far as the image of Brunelleschi as machine builder and machine inventor is reflected by the record known to us today, it shows an architect-engineer who developed the mechanical elements then

---

[12] A general orientation is offered by L. White, "Pumps and Pendula: Galileo and Technology," *Galileo Reappraised,* ed. C. L. Golino, Berkeley, 1966.

available into a highly refined system. He controlled the building and working of this system with iron willpower and rigid secrecy. By this remarkable *tour de force* he contributed little to the progress of machinery, but he contributed greatly to his personal success and that of his main work, the Cupola. As in his building method, which was free of various conventional expedients, he demonstrated once more the possibility of individual progress, beyond limits stipulated by ancient rules.

The biographers say that features of Roman ruins suggested to him the use of stone hanger tools, known in Roman times. It is possible that this was so, and it is even possible that he personally so informed Manetti. However, we think the hangers are secondary to his machinery, and his pertinent discoveries are secondary to the history of his mechanical conceptions and innovations. In a more significant way these innovations had nothing to do with Rome, Antiquity, and the Renaissance. They are part of the effort of a Gothic master, operating in his Gothic world. It may be for this reason that they were promptly forgotten. They were ingenious, but they belonged to a world then about to disappear, not to the world of his real successors or of his own major enterprises as architect.

CONCLUSIONS

When the Florentines buried Filippo in the Cathedral that he had substantially completed for them, they asked his pupil and adopted son Andrea il Buggiano to show his likeness in marble and below it they wrote,

> How Filippo the architect excelled in invention is shown not only by the beautiful shell of this famous temple but also by various machines that he invented with divine genius. . . .

Ever since then he was known as a most remarkable engineer and as the man who worked most outstandingly in one architectural style while laying the foundations of another. In our opinion he was one of the great developers of building principles for all times.

Before him there had been an impasse in Florentine architecture.

Romanesque and Gothic builders had proposed and debated ambitious plans, but only the Gothic masters had specified clear ideas about a possible way of execution of the plans, and one basic part of their formula, the use of outer buttresses, had been vetoed by the Romanesque masters.

A full return to Gothic forms and methods, for the construction of supports of the Cupola, was proposed by Giovanni d'Ambrogio, who directed the work during the first eighteen years of the Quattrocento. Brunelleschi's Cupola structure is different from that suggested by Giovanni, but even in Brunelleschi's work there is considerable Gothic influence. Far from using a single tradition, either in statics or ornamentation, his Cupola uses a structure and form wherein Gothic and Classic elements are synthesized. This fact is often overlooked. It is misleading to call Filippo merely the renewer of an ancient form.[13]

The history of the building demonstrates the recurrence of medieval and ancient traditions and the master's achievement in uniting them. In 1404, the tall buttresses and windows of Giovanni d'Ambrogio were rejected, but the lower buttress elements shown by the model of his predecessors were retained. This was done by a group that included Brunelleschi and Ghiberti. A few years later the Florentine Tambour was designed, approved, and built by new groups of men, whose identity is less clearly documented. According to eminent writers, Brunelleschi was influential (again). We think there is good evidence in support of this view, and there is no good evidence against it. We may conclude that Filippo, Lorenzo, and perhaps others, jointly opposing Giovanni d'Ambrogio, established a wide spatial separation between the compromise features used in the understructure and a new, higher, independent Cupola. Like the artists of 1367, these men vetoed a conventional Gothic form, without showing exactly what form was to be substituted. It was not necessarily a form totally devoid of Gothic features.

Soon after completion of the Tambour and of some model work

[13] As mentioned by Sanpaolesi, pp. 110f. [*Brunelleschi*, Milan, 1962; and see below, p. 152.—Ed.], Filippo brought about a repudiation of Gothic art. However, as noted by Sanpaolesi, p. 31, Filippo himself was interested in Gothic-influenced statics. A similar view is stated, although unclearly, by P. Frankl, *Die Renaissance-Architektur in Italien*, Leipzig, 1912, p. 2. In fact, as indicated in these studies, Filippo contributed creatively to traditions in statics which are of a peculiarly Gothic character.

for statues to be placed in lower regions of the Dome, or perhaps after abandonment of work on these statues, Filippo showed the form to be used for the Cupola and began to persuade the builders to adopt it— a process that lasted from 1417 to 1420. He proposed to construct the large vault as a double shell reinforced by ribs and small arches; these were modified Gothic buttresses and hollow ribs. He combined them with tie rings; these were modified Roman features. He fully overcame the former hesitations of the Florentines and persuaded them to adopt the new design, which he then used with singular success in building the Cupola during the next twelve years. He also began to produce final details, including the Classic-Gothic design for the Lantern crowning the Cupola. His structure solved the static problems that he had inherited, and foreshadowed basic modern principles of construction. It gave timeless expression to a new architectural principle—a major addition to the other architectural innovations introduced by Filippo. At the outset of these studies we were not sure whether Brunelleschi's achievement was as great as his friends asserted. We are now inclined to think that he may have been more creative as a builder than most of his admirers imagined.

Filippo also devised mechanical systems for delivering, hoisting, and placing the building materials. Some of these devices may have contributed to the progress of machinery and surely they contributed much to his personal fame, as they allowed him to build with remarkable speed and safety. His mechanical inventions also had side effects in the evolution of patents. The machines were admired, and their success gave confidence to other mechanics.

We have tried to develop an image of Brunelleschi the builder and engineer, but had to disregard many facets of his remarkable personality, such as his contacts with goldsmiths, sculptors, and painters. We are able to cite only two personal, verbal statements of Brunelleschi the man—a sonnet deriding a critic and a speech addressed to a friend. We see him use playful superiority over his critic and hear him talk to his friend about the people at large with a strange mixture of sarcasm and rage. The biographers add, credibly, that he spoke freely with common people and, for a purpose, with men of property and influence; that he hated his rival; and that he made his points with single-mindedness and insistence. In his specification for the Cupola he makes his points in nearly perfect form. Our impression is that his powers came from what he saw rather than from that which others could tell him.

Brunelleschi's work, together with the work of direct followers, almost totally transformed the artistic traditions of Quattrocento builders. His influence on building technique may have been comparable in depth, if not in rapidity. However, much remains to be studied in this technical area.[14]

The engineering work of the Renaissance began to be studied near the end of the eighteenth century, when G. B. Venturi rediscovered the "mathematical-physical" works of Leonardo, together with those of Taccola. Since then many documents relating to such works have been found. The hero worship and anecdotal accounts of early biographers then fell into some disrepute. However, we must not be too harsh with the biographers. The rediscovered record proves that interesting beginnings were disregarded by them but not that Filippo's life and work was significantly different from the pattern established by the early reports. The biographers and their informants among the common people did not use words of precise definition—nor did the early architects and notaries do so when they produced the documents, rediscovered in recent times. Only when official documents, engineering notebooks, or biographies independently corroborate one another do these records gain more than the limited evidentiary value that each of them inherently has.

The studies undertaken here, using biographies, drawing records, and official documents, have led us to the conclusion that many historic processes came under Brunelleschi's influence. We hope that future historians will consider his time and work in a comprehensive way. We find the effort rewarding, even if the conclusions remain tentative. When we first undertook our studies, we were ignorant of several Brunelleschian reports that now are frequently mentioned, and many such reports are still imperfectly known. The notes of Taccola, Ghiberti, and Leonardo are among them, aside from those of Alberti, Francesco di Giorgio, the San Gallos, and many others. The study of

---

[14] See the references to civil and mechanical engineering in the chart presented at the end of this book [not reproduced in this reprinting—Ed.]. It outlines pathways of Brunelleschian influence, as they appear to us from these studies. Each name listed in the chart stands for many concepts proposed or elaborated or transmitted; few of the details have been studied thus far.

some such reports alerted us to interesting facts and challenging problems. Even so we are not sure that we have found more than a sampling of what can be found on further research. Records of several centuries remain to be reread and reevaluated. Their study should help us, gradually, understand more of the growth of architecture and technical science brought about by Brunelleschi and his contemporaries.

Piero Sanpaolesi
"Notes Towards an Appraisal
of the Man and His Work,"
in *Brunelleschi* (1962)

An appraisal of Brunelleschi's personality can be only a brief glimpse of some fundamental aspects of his spirit seen against the background of his times. His freedom of invention emerges above all; it allies him with the most fertile of experimenters by his capacity to acquire the data and premises of a wide cultural panorama rapidly and profoundly. They intimately penetrate his spirit and become the instruments of his action, which finds its greatest stimulus in the conviction he puts into these acquisitions. Therefore he is fundamentally a free agent in search of laws to which he can conform according to his own moral standard. The coherence of his every act is a result of this, as is the coherence of every one of his forms, from his very first work of sculpture to the last architectural achievements of his full maturity! In fact, Brunelleschi died at the peak of his maximum *inventive capacity*. His mental process seems to follow a prevalently inductive pattern common to many men of great genius confronting

From P. Sanpaolesi, *Brunelleschi* (Milan: Edizione per il Club del Libro, 1962), pp. 110–15. Reprinted by permission of the author. Translated by Beverly Levine. Footnotes by the Editor.

natural facts and history (understood also as a natural fact). It moves from an analytic attitude provided by his acute observation of facts and phenomena, to an urgent cognitive need. On this analytic process he bases his convictions. Proceeding this way with formal factors as well as scientific factors, he reduces them to a common denominator —knowledge. To have had enough conviction to be able to provoke by himself the repudiation of the forms (tired though they were) of Gothic art in order to turn to classic forms, is an act of will similar in magnitude to the founding of an empire. But it is not an isolated act. The probing into the nature of the various mathematical and figurative aspects of a formal problem then leads him to perspective, another empire where he is the lawmaker, and to experiments in statics and mechanics, already premonitions of extraordinary developments.

All these activities are also expressed poetically throughout his architectural works. In these geometry and arithmetic are equally present, but the sense of proportion, the rhythm, the color, and the use of lighting simultaneously satisfy the intellectual and therefore historical components, as well as those which are universal and transcend the ages. We, then, while we still feel able to participate in this historicism only to some degree, nonetheless enjoy his structures with a singular freshness and perception—they are still lovely and youthful in spirit, still as rich with instruction for us as for those who saw them built. These works transport us beyond temporal contingencies each time we ask them to. The beauty of the Brunelleschian structures does not reside in the formal perfection of their parts but in the perfection and harmony of the whole. A wooden model such as that for the Lantern of the Cupola, though it may contain no definition of details, can take the place of the constructed architecture because it is extraordinarily rich in form and conception, fused to the ineffable that is poetry. . . .

The fact that he had always preferred to make use of models rather than drawings to plan his buildings shows Brunelleschi's predilection for synthesizing individual parts. This intellectual process reveals that his interest was aimed primarily at the whole organism rather than the individual forms of its members. All the same, these forms do not lose their important modular function but, as they are implicit to the inventive synthesis, they regulate the growth and modular organization of it at the very moment of invention. The building comes from his hands as a whole and never as an aggregate of parts. He never attempts in any case to reconstruct the total form of antique structures, but ventures upon an original elaboration of their modular system.

This is the fundamental reason for his freedom. In fact, Brunelleschi does not imitatively transfer forms learned externally and superficially; instead, as a profoundly cultured man, he elaborates the data of a culture congenial to him. If he had been tightly bound to the traditional use of antique orders (even though reconstructed by him within their own modular laws), he would have had to adopt antique organisms as well, and such an attitude on his part would have led him not to experimentation with new structures and laws but to a neoclassicism.

His interpretation of the facts of nature is always made from a universal point of view. His perspective is not a process for those painters who wish to represent natural things in space, but it is a new way of seeing and interpreting nature—as valuable, therefore, for architects as for musicians, for sculptors as for poets.

His personality could not help but be subject to the highs and lows of both boundless admiration and the sharpest criticism. He was terribly witty, and a joker, and his tongue knew no obstacles when it came to passing judgment or taking part in a prank. From "the peasant on a cross" of the Donatellian Crucifix to the "have him do another of them and he will do mine" of carpenter [Antonio di Manetto Ciaccheri's] model for the Lantern of S. Maria del Fiore, to the answer given to someone who asked what was the best thing Ghiberti had ever done ("to sell Lepriano," a rocky little farm that Ghiberti had only recently got rid of), to the principal role he played in the atrocious trick on Il Grasso, his ability to be right on target with a judgment, and his satisfaction at his sure success in this game at which he felt himself so able—all are coherent aspects of his need for freedom.[1] It was fortunate for him that this feeling was then still widespread and dominant in Florence, and that no wearing

---

[1] [The anecdotes referred to in this sentence may be found in Antonio Manetti's *The Life of Brunelleschi,* ed. Saalman, pp. 112, 62, 129 n. 2; and in Giorgio Vasari's biography of Brunelleschi in the *Lives . . . ,* ed. Everyman's Library, I, 273, 299.]

political or doctrinal bond deterred him. This same freedom also led him to accept an incredible mass of work, all the more oppressive if one bears in mind that he personally directed all the projects without helpers, continuously staying on the site wherever there was need of him, always supervising. His ideas certainly did not come while he sat at his desk but rather sprang one from the other in the continual working experience, flanked by his search for models, antique or otherwise, as long as they were stimulating and suitable to his geometric standard of interpreting structural forms. He was an extraordinary inventor, of architecture above all; but wherever he put his hand he drew forth a spring of energy, and stimulated new forms and procedures with his experiments.

Death cut off Brunelleschi's creative activity abruptly; he was like one who, working with his own hands and continually deepening and broadening his vision and experience, was reborn, so to speak, every day. And there was no one who could replace him in carrying out and planning works.

When Brunelleschi was an old man, his experiences found hardly an echo among those who at other times had been his followers—Michelozzo, Manetti, Giuliano da Maiano, Salvi d'Andrea—and their work shows it. Some of his ideas remained universally accepted and widespread, but his last forms—the Lantern of S. Maria del Fiore, the Pazzi Chapel as he left it at his death (with the extrados of the barrel vaults visible, and without the portico that was added later);[2] Santo Spirito, covered with a barrel vault rather than a flat ceiling;[3] and finally Santa Maria degli Angeli, of which I have made a hypothetical reconstruction[4]—fell into the oblivion in which they have substantially remained until today. These late works show Brunelleschi headed for and almost having arrived at that conceptual maturation of the structural organism where syntactic uncertainties have disappeared and there are no longer any little compromises (some can still be seen in the Pazzi Chapel—the slice of pilaster in the

---

[2] [See original text, pp. 82ff. and text figs. E and F. Also see G. Laschi, P. Roselli, P. A. Ricci, "Indagine sulla Capella dei Pazzi," *Commentari*, XIII (1962), 24–41.]

[3] [See original text, p. 64 and text fig. D. Also see L. Benevolo, S. Chieffi, G. Mezzetti, "Indagine sul S. Spirito di Brunelleschi," *Quaderni dell'Istituto di Storia dell' Architettura* Series XV, Fasc. 85–90 (1968), pp. 1–52.]

[4] [See original text, pp. 88f. and text fig. H.]

corner, for example). This maturity is also manifest in the Lantern of Santa Maria del Fiore, a completed structure on which he conferred only a formal finish freeing it from any practical function. It seems that by then he had dissipated any self-doubt about his necessary freedom or the limits to his creation of new forms. He had only partially acquired this freedom when, ignoring the indefiniteness and the fantasy of the Gothic mode, he accepted the measurement of space according to perspective and the antique orders. At a certain point even these are a hindrance if they are not regarded simply as orders but as schematically prearranged total structures. He takes a stand against the laws set down in Hellenistic-Roman architecture, as Late Roman and Byzantine architects had, in their time, passed from the rigid rectangular scheme to complex forms and finally, to the double shell designs.

Nevertheless, these Brunelleschian ideas, or portions of them, are manifest in three buildings which are not his. The Chapel of the Crucifix in San Miniato al Monte by Michelozzo, the Cardini Chapel in San Francesco in Pescia by his adopted son and heir, Il Buggiano, and the Badia in Fiesole attributed to Brunelleschi by Vasari (although it was built fifteen years after his death) all contain suggestions of Brunelleschi's late activity. In any case, barrel-vaulted coverings instead of flat roofs exist in all three of these structures. In the Chapel of the Crucifix and in San Francesco in Pescia the extrados of these vaults is also visible, as was intended in the lateral vaults of the Pazzi Chapel. On the other hand, the entire Cardini Chapel repeats the scheme of [Masaccio's] *Trinity* in Santa Maria Novella as if to give new evidence, in constructed space, of that imagined space.[5]

I have already said that the most direct acceptance of late Brunelleschian forms is found in Lombardy and Emilia. [Alessio] Tramello in Piacenza seems almost to have come from Brunelleschi's own workshop as far as spatial perspective conceptions are concerned, and perhaps first Filarete and then Leonardo spread throughout Milan the forms of Brunelleschi's late activity which are continually recalled in the designs of both artists. That form of the decoratively turned column which had been used so long by [Giovanni Antonio] Amadeo in Lombardy and which was then transferred by [Mauro] Codussi

[5] [See original text, pp. 51ff. and text fig. C.]

to Venice and Padua (note the house in Via delle Torreselle in Padua), descends from the prototype of the turned cylinders of the Lantern of Santa Maria del Fiore. Even the details of a typical Lombard building such as the Colleoni Chapel at Bergamo—from the polychromaticism of the windows, to the crown of small aligned niches, to the large [polygonal vault] (the first extradosal cupola in Lombardy)—are all present in the late works of Brunelleschi and evidently had migrated to northern Italy.

At this point our awareness will become more concrete if we cast an attentive glance at the works of Alessio Tramello at Piacenza, and especially at many of their details such as the plans of San Sisto and San Sepolcro, with niches evident on the exterior, the curious paired windows of San Sepolcro, and the vaulted and small domed coverings of the interiors. But one church in the hills of Florence, the Badia of Fiesole, has been at times both attributed and denied to Brunelleschi. The fact remains that the few documents regarding its construction (or completion?) date back [only] to 1462 and some years following, and this is certainly a weighty argument. Moreover, from these documents the name of Francesco di Simone Ferrucci emerges together with that of Giuliano da Maiano; we can also find the names of minor masters, Lombards, among whom could be those called by Brunelleschi to build the Cupola of Santa Maria del Fiore, or their descendants. Even though many years had passed since the death of Brunelleschi, we find ourselves still surrounded by his followers. While Ferrucci remains a very accomplished carver of Fiesolian stones, Giuliano becomes a most original architect. Among his works, the Duomo of Faenza is enough to remind us of his ties to Brunelleschi. The Duomo of Faenza, in fact, is covered by sail vaults; the Badia of Fiesole is covered by a great barrel vault which is interrupted at the crossing of the transept, and at that point it is not a cross vault that rises but a sail vault. The thrust of the barrel vault is borne by the rather high walls on which it is carried, and these in turn are supported by the partition walls of the chapels that rise high enough to be reinforcements. Here then we are in the presence of a Brunelleschian element to which [Filippo] would have given a visible solution, but which has instead very much encumbered the builders. They felt constrained to enclose these buttresses in an envelope of stone walls that, void of architecturally appreciable forms as it is, demonstrates that they did not know how to realize someone else's design. This design goes back by well-founded hypotheses only to one hand—that of Brunelleschi.

Not one of the structures of Brunelleschi's maturity is, therefore, brought to a good end, except perhaps the Lantern of Santa Maria del Fiore. Regret for so many incomplete works is thus not merely rhetorical.

One hundred and fifty years before Brunelleschi was born, Roger Bacon wrote:

> It is possible to make Engines so that either fresh or salt water vessels may be guided by the help of one man and made to sail with a greater swiftness than others which are full of men to help them. . . . It is possible to make a Chariot move with an inestimable swiftness . . . without the help of any living creature. . . . It is possible to invent an Engine of little bulk yet of great efficacy either to the depressing or elevation of the very greatest weight. . . .[6]

Brunelleschi did not write any of that, but he did it, not empirically, but by proceeding from precise theoretical premises.

[6] [Quoted here in the English translation cited in H. Stanley Redgrove, *Roger Bacon*, London, 1920, pp. 58f.]

1377	Born in Florence, the second of three sons of notary Ser Brunellesco di Lippo Lapi and Giuliana degli Spini
1398	Applied for registration as a goldsmith in the Silk Guild (*Arte della Seta*)
1399–1400	Employed as a goldsmith-sculptor on the silver altar in S. Jacopo, Pistoia
1401	Entered contest for Baptistery Door reliefs, Florence, along with Lorenzo Ghiberti and five other sculptors. Trial panel, bronze relief of *The Sacrifice of Isaac* (Bargello, Florence)
1402	Lorenzo Ghiberti declared winner of contest
1404	Matriculated in the Silk Guild as a Master
	Earliest association with the overseers of Florence Cathedral, as a member of a committee to give advice on one of the buttresses for the building
?ca.1410–15	Rediscovered principles of linear perspective construction, demonstrated with two painted panels (now lost) of Florentine streets and buildings
1415	Together with Donatello produced a model for a statue intended for Florence Cathedral but never executed
1417	First official record of work on Cupola matters—received payment for designs and labor
	Adopted Andrea di Lazzaro Cavalcanti, called Il Buggiano, a child of five, and took him into his household
ca.1418	Commissioned by Giovanni di Bicci de' Medici to build the Old Sacristy, S. Lorenzo

1418	Submitted a model for the Cupola, to be constructed without armature
1419	Received payment for a model of the Cupola Lantern
	Construction of the Ospedale degli Innocenti begun
1420	Brunelleschi's Cupola model, selected by the overseers of the Cathedral
	Brunelleschi, Ghiberti, and Battista d'Antonio appointed joint *capomaestri* of the Cupola
	Construction of the Cupola begun
1420s	Construction begun on Brunelleschi's addition to the Palazzo della Parte Guelfa, probably completed by Francesco della Luna
1421	Brunelleschi's name appeared in the records of the Ospedale degli Innocenti for the first time; his name appeared for the last time in 1426; in 1427 changes in the original design were made by Francesco della Luna
	Awarded 100 florins for designing a complex hoisting machine for use in the construction of the Cupola
	Awarded with a monopoly patent for the invention of a transport ship to carry building supplies
	Construction of the Old Sacristy of S. Lorenzo begun
	Construction of the church of S. Lorenzo begun; building campaigns, 1421–25, ca.1429, 1441–1460s
1423	Named *"inventor et ghubernator"* of the Cupola
	Awarded another prize for an addition to his hoisting machine of 1421
1426	In Pisa working on fortifications
1429–30	Contracted by the Pazzi family to build a chapter-house (Pazzi Chapel) for the monks of S. Croce in the S. Croce cloister. Construction possibly not begun until 1442; still unfinished in the 1460s
1430	Failure of river deflection strategy in war with Lucca
	Advice sought on fortifications in Rencine, Staggia, Castellina
1434	Design for S. Spirito (or 1428, depending on interpretation of the documents)
	S. Maria degli Angeli begun for the Camaldolese Monastery; left unfinished in 1437
	Jailed for eleven days over jurisdictional dispute with the Stonemasons' and Woodworkers' Guild
1435	In Pisa, working on fortifications

?ca.1435–40	Invention of stage machinery for Annunciation play performed in S. Felice in Piazza
1436	Cupola completed and consecrated
	Design for Cupola Lantern, revised from rough model of 1419, accepted
	Foundations begun at S. Spirito; work continued through 1480s
	In Vicopisano working on fortifications
1439	Model for the Exedrae of Florence Cathedral approved; first Exedra completed in 1445, the remaining three in the 1460s
1440	In Pisa working on fortifications
1443	Received payment for a wooden model for a marble pulpit in S. Maria Novella; pulpit executed after Brunelleschi's death by Andrea di Lazzaro Cavalcanti
1446	Death; body temporarily interred in the Campanile of Florence Cathedral
1447	Burial in Florence Cathedral

• • •

Architectural Works in progress at the time of Brunelleschi's death:

S. Lorenzo; S. Spirito; Pazzi Chapel; Lantern of the Cupola; three of the four Exedrae of the Cathedral.

Controversial attributed architectural works:

Palazzo Pitti; Badia, Fiesole; Palazzo Bardi-Busini; Barbadori Chapel, S. Felicita.

Sculpture attributed:

Figures of prophets and church fathers on the silver altar, S. Jacopo, Pistoia; wood crucifix, Gondi Chapel, S. Maria Novella; Polychrome terracotta *tondi* of the four evangelists, Pazzi Chapel, S. Croce.

Sculpture lost:

Polychrome wood statue of Mary Magdalene, S. Spirito.

Notes on the Editor and Contributors

Isabelle Hyman is Associate Professor of Fine Arts at Washington Square College, New York University. She received a B.A. from Vassar College in 1951, an M.A. from Columbia University in 1955, and from New York University (Institute of Fine Arts) an M.A. in 1966 and a Ph.D. in 1968. Her work has been concentrated on fifteenth-century Florentine architecture. In 1972–73 she was Samuel H. Kress Senior Fellow at Villa I Tatti, The Harvard University Center for Italian Resaissance Studies, in Florence.

Leon Battista Alberti (1404–1472). Exemplar of the "Renaissance man," Alberti distinguished himself as a precocious and gifted writer, theorist, architect, historian, scientist, and humanist. His treaties on painting, sculpture, and especially architecture established the theoretical foundations of Early Renaissance art. He was born, illegitimately, into an aristocratic Florentine family in exile. He was educated and worked in Padua, Bologna, Rome, Florence, Rimini, Mantua, and traveled elsewhere in Italy and abroad. He knew Brunelleschi personally, and admired the avant-garde art of early quattrocento Florence. The most famous structures designed by Alberti, San Francesco in Rimini and San Andrea in Mantua, set Renaissance architecture on a new course.

Francesco Bocchi (1548–1618). Active in the literary life of Florence in the later sixteenth century, Francesco Bocchi produced books and essays on a wide variety of subjects, including art and music. His *Le Bellezze della città di Fiorenza*, the first substantial guidebook to Florence, was published in 1591 and extols the artistic excellence of his city.

Andrea di Lazzaro Cavalcanti (Il Buggiano) (1412–1462). Andrea di Lazzaro Cavalcanti, known as Il Buggiano because his birthplace was Borgo a Buggiano, near Pescia, was adopted at the age of five by Filippo

163

Brunelleschi, and eventually became his heir. Probably trained and launched into the Florentine art world by Brunelleschi, Buggiano worked mostly as a sculptor and sometimes as an architect during the 1430s, 40s, and 50s. He paid tribute to his years with Brunelleschi by requesting (and receiving) after the architect's death the commission to carve Brunelleschi's tomb relief.

Giovanni Cavalcanti (first half of the fifteenth century). Nothing is known about this fifteenth-century chronicler of Florence apart from a few personal references that he includes in his *History of Florence*. Written around 1440 while Cavalcanti was in prison for debt, the *History* is a mixture of fact, gossip, and opinion from the point of view of a sceptical and uninhibited reporter.

Pope Eugenius IV (reigned 1431–1447). Gabriele Condulmer was born of a noble Venetian family in 1383. He joined the Augustinian order and was made Bishop of Siena and then Cardinal by his uncle, Pope Gregory XII. He was elected to the Papacy, as Eugenius IV, in 1431, and his reign was marked by the turbulance of the Basel Council, revolution, and exile. He fled from Rome in 1434 and took refuge in Florence. There he knew Filippo Brunelleschi, and consecrated the Cathedral in 1436 after Brunelleschi's Dome was completed.

Cornel von Fabriczy (1839–1910). Born in Leutschau, Hungary, in 1839, Fabriczy went to Germany to study engineering when he was a young man. Until 1870 he had an active career as an engineer, and he was responsible for the construction of important railway works in Germany and Hungary. After 1870 he was increasingly drawn to study and research in the new field of art history, and he retired to Stuttgart, interrupting his study and writing only for research trips to other cities, principally Florence and Venice. He devoted himself to the study of Tuscan Renaissance architecture and sculpture, and to Venetian sculpture. In 1892 he published his major work, the biography of Brunelleschi, which was the result of his profound studies in the archives of Florence and of the monuments themselves.

Hans Folnesics (1887–1922). Illness cut short the life and career of Viennese art historian Hans Folnesics. After completing his studies under Max Dvořák, Folnesics served as *Landeskonservator* in Salzburg but retired from that post in 1917 as a result of ill health. His contributions to art history were made in the field of fifteenth-century Italian architecture and sculpture; his monograph on Brunelleschi was published in 1915.

Paolo Fontana (1865–1944). Paolo Fontana was born in Lerici, in the province of Liguria, in 1865. Beginning in 1903, he was Professor of *Lettere* at the Accademia di Belle Arti in Florence where he taught art history. During the more than a quarter of a century that he taught at that institution, he published numerous studies in the history of architecture, concentrating particularly on the works of Brunelleschi.

Lorenzo Ghiberti (1378–1455). One of the dominant figures in Florentine sculpture in the first half of the fifteenth century, Lorenzo Ghiberti was first trained as a goldsmith and painter. In 1401 he entered the competition for the Baptistery Door and was the victor over Brunelleschi and five other contestants. A bitter rivalry between the two men dates from this incident, although they were forced to collaborate on some aspects of the construction of the Dome of Florence Cathedral. Ghiberti's *Commentarii*, written in the 1440s, includes an autobiography in which he sets down his version of the Baptistery Door contest.

Giovanni di Gherardo da Prato (1367–ca.1444). Active in humanist circles in Florence in the first decades of the fifteenth century, Giovanni di Gherardo da Prato was, like his colleagues, a man of many parts. He was born in Prato and studied law at the University of Padua. In addition to practicing law in Florence, he lectured on Dante at the University of Florence, wrote poetry, and was consultant and designer for civic architectural projects, particularly the construction of the Cathedral Dome, where his hostility to Brunelleschi probably developed.

Ludwig H. Heydenreich. Born in Leipzig in 1903, Ludwig H. Heydenreich studied the history of art and classical archeology at the universities of Berlin and Hamburg with Adolf Goldschmidt, Erwin Panofsky, Fritz Saxl, and Aby Warburg. After he received his Ph.D. in 1928, he studied and traveled extensively in Italy, and also in England and France. In 1948 he became director of the newly founded Zentralinstitut für Kunstgeschichte in Munich, and remained in that post until his retirement in 1970. His many publications include studies of Leonardo da Vinci and Italian Renaissance architecture. He has lectured widely throughout Europe and the United States.

Richard Krautheimer. Distinguished scholar and teacher, Richard Krautheimer has written and lectured on almost all epochs in the history of art from antiquity to the present. Educated in Munich, Berlin, and Halle, he received his doctorate *summa cum laude* from the University of Halle in 1923. Emigrating to the United States in 1935, Dr. Krautheimer taught at the University of Louisville, Kentucky, Vassar College, and the Institute of Fine Arts of New York University, where in 1965 he was named Jayne Wrightsman Professor of Fine Arts. Among his many highly praised articles and books, *Lorenzo Ghiberti*, which he wrote in collaboration with Trude Krautheimer-Hesse, stands out as an exemplary scholarly achievement.

Cristoforo Landino (1424–1492). A Florentine of humble origins, Cristoforo Landino, through Medici patronage and his own outstanding abilities as a writer and classical scholar, became one of the eminent humanists in the orbit around Lorenzo de' Medici, Il Magnifico. In 1458 he was elected to the chair of poetry and oratory in the University of Florence; in 1467 he was appointed secretary of the Guelf Party; and in 1481 wrote his famous commentary to Dante's *Divine Comedy*, the introduction to which contained a brief section on artists, including Brunelleschi.

Niccolò Machiavelli (1469–1527). Florentine statesman, writer, and political thinker, Niccolò Machiavelli entered public affairs as second chancellor of the republic in 1498, and carried out important diplomatic missions in Italy and abroad. He wrote treatises on statecraft, history, military reform, and war; his best-known work is the *Prince*, written in 1513. From 1520 to 1525 Machiavelli wrote a history of Florence in which he contemptuously described the failure of Brunelleschi's scheme to defeat Lucca in the war of 1430.

Antonio di Tuccio Manetti (1423–1497). It is now generally agreed that the anonymous author of the *Vita* of Brunelleschi can be identified as Antonio di Tuccio Manetti, Florentine citizen active in public life, letters, and architecture (see H. Saalman, ed., *The Life of Brunelleschi*, pp. 10ff.). In his youth Manetti was an acquaintance of the older Brunelleschi, whom he idolized; he wrote his adulatory biography in the 1480s, after Brunelleschi had been dead for four decades. Manetti is also believed to be the author of *XIV Uomini Singhularii in Firenze*, written between 1494 and 1497 as an appendix to an Italian translation of Filippo Villani's *De famosis civibus* (see P. Murray, *Burlington Magazine*, 99 [1957], 330f.).

Francesco Milizia (1725–1798). Born in 1725 in Oria in the province of Otranto, a part of the Kingdom of Naples, Francesco Milizia was educated in Padua and Naples, first studying literature and later "mathematics, medicine, logic, and metaphysics," as he reports in his autobiographical memoir. After he had settled down to "scientific pursuits," a visit to Rome directed his interest to architecture. In Rome he became part of the neoclassic world around Mengs and Winckelmann, and he was appointed superintendent of buildings in the Papal See for the King of the Two Sicilies. He also published a number of theoretical works on architecture and art, as well as his popular *Le Vite de' più celebri architetti* (1768), which reflects his knowledge of the writings of French neoclassical theorist Marc-Antoine Laugier.

Carlo Marsuppini (1398–1453). Born in Arezzo to a wealthy mercantile family, Carlo Marsuppini became one of the foremost humanist intellectuals in the Medici circle in Florence during the first half of the fifteenth century. He had a brilliant public career which began with his appointment in 1431 as lecturer at the University of Florence. In 1444 he succeeded humanist Lionardo Bruni in the illustrious position of state chancellor of Florence. Brunelleschi's importance in the republic in 1446, the year of his death, can be attested by the selection of the prestigious Marsuppini, with his renowned gifts in classical languages, rhetoric, and poetry, to compose the epitaph for Brunelleschi's tomb.

Charles Herbert Moore (1840–1930).   American writer, teacher, and artist, Charles Herbert Moore was born in New York City in 1840, taught fine arts and design at Harvard University beginning in 1871, in 1895 became curator of the Fogg Art Museum, and in 1896 its director. Strongly influenced by John Ruskin, Moore made intensive studies of medieval architecture which resulted in a series of books, principally *Development and Character of Gothic Architecture* (1890). In 1905 Moore published *Character of Renaissance Architecture*, in which he expresses sharp criticism of the forms and structure of the architecture of the Renaissance.

Frank D. Prager.   Born in Munich in 1907, Frank D. Prager was educated in law and engineering before emigrating to the United States in 1935. He received his law degree from the University of Munich in 1930, and worked as a patent attorney in the United States, where a developing interest in the history of patents led him to his studies of Brunelleschi. Since then he has published many articles on Brunelleschi's technology, and is co-author with Gustina Scaglia of *Brunelleschi, Studies of His Technology and Inventions* (1970).

Giovanni Rucellai (1403–1481).   Giovanni Rucellai was a wealthy Florentine merchant related through marriage to the prominent and powerful families of Cosimo de' Medici and Palla Strozzi. A patriotic and responsible citizen who served Florence during the 1460s and 70s through his election to various public offices, Rucellai was noted also for his charitable donations and his patronage of artist Leon Battista Alberti. The *Zibaldone Quaresimale*, Rucellai's memoirs (in which he pays tribute to the reputation of Brunelleschi), are a valuable source for studies of fifteenth-century Florentine life.

John Ruskin (1819–1900).   Author, art critic, poet, lecturer, and social reformer, John Ruskin was one of the great intellectuals of nineteenth-century England. He won the Newdigate Prize for poetry in 1839, and soon after began to write on painting, architecture, and economics. From 1870 to 1879 and from 1883 to 1884 he was Slade Professor of Art at Oxford. Deeply moralistic, he searched for connections between art and morality, believing that he found them expressed most perfectly in medieval art.

Howard Saalman.   Howard Saalman is Andrew H. Mellon Professor of Architecture at Carnegie-Mellon University in Pittsburgh, where he has been teaching since 1958. Educated at the City College of New York (A.B. 1949) and the Institute of Fine Arts, New York University (M.A. 1955, Ph.D. 1960), Dr. Saalman has concentrated his studies on the architectural history of medieval and Renaissance Florence, and the evolution of urban form. His book *Haussmann: Paris Transformed* appeared in 1971. He is currently at work on a two-volume monograph on the architecture of Brunelleschi and the Cupola of Santa Maria del Fiore, the Cathedral of Florence.

Piero Sanpaolesi. Distinguished Professor in the Faculty of Architecture of the Università degli Studi in Florence, Piero Sanpaolesi is the Director of its Istituto di Restauro dei Monumenti. He has published many books and articles on Italian Renaissance sculpture and architecture, and has specialized in studies of Brunelleschi and his works.

Gustina Scaglia. Gustina Scaglia is Professor of the history of art at Queens College, City University of New York. She was born in Glastonbury, Connecticut, and received her Ph.D. in 1961 from New York University (Institute of Fine Arts). Her studies of Brunelleschian machines began with her dissertation on the *Zibaldone* of Buonaccorso Ghiberti. In addition to *Brunelleschi, Studies of His Technology and Inventions* (as co-author with Frank D. Prager), she has recently published two books: Mariano Taccola, *De Machinis* and (with Frank D. Prager) *Mariano Taccola and His Book "De ingenesis."*

Geoffrey Scott (1885–1929). Writer and architect, Geoffrey Scott was born in England in 1885 and was educated at Oxford. His best-known work, *The Architecture of Humanism* (1914), combined his literary talent with his interest in Renaissance architecture. His familiarity with Italian architecture developed during his years in Florence when he was one of two designers selected to remodel Bernard Berenson's villa, I Tatti. He died in New York City in 1929 while at work editing a collection of Boswell's papers.

Mariano di Jacopo Taccola (1382–ca.1454). Born in Siena in 1382, Mariano di Jacopo Taccola was an engineer, a writer on technology, a notary, a sculptor, and was known in his own time as "the Sienese Archimedes." He is the author of an illustrated technical treatise, *De Machinis*, written in 1449, and of *De ingeneis* of 1433 recently identified by G. Scaglia and F. D. Prager (see Mariano Taccola, *De machinis*, ed. G. Scaglia, Wiesbaden, 1971, I, p. 7, 9, n. 1). A mutual interest in technology brought him together with Brunelleschi in the years around 1425.

Giorgio Vasari (1511–1574). Versatile artist and writer, Giorgio Vasari was born in Arezzo and trained first as a painter in Florence. There he enjoyed the friendship of Michelangelo, the patronage of the Medici family, and worked as an architect as well as a painter. His most famous and important work is literary—the *Vite de' piu eccellenti Architetti, Pittori, e Scultori . . .* , dedicated to the Medici Duke Cosimo I, published first in 1550 and then in an enlarged edition in 1568. In addition to his biographies of artists the book contains Vasari's explanation of the development of Renaissance art.

Selected Bibliography

BRUNELLESCHI SCULPTOR

KRAUTHEIMER, R., with T. KRAUTHEIMER-HESS. *Lorenzo Ghiberti,* 2nd ed. Princeton, 1970. I, 44ff.

POPE-HENNESSY, J. *Italian Renaissance Sculpture.* London, 1958, pp. 267–68.

SANPAOLESI, P. "Aggiunte al Brunelleschi." In *Bollettino d'Arte,* 37 (1953), 225–32.

SEYMOUR, C. JR. *Sculpture in Italy 1400–1500.* Baltimore, 1966.

SHAPLEY, F. R., and C. KENNEDY. "Brunelleschi in Competition with Ghiberti." In *Art Bulletin,* 5 (1922–23), 31–34.

BRUNELLESCHI AND PERSPECTIVE

ARGAN, G. C. "The Architecture of Brunelleschi and the Origins of Perspective Theory." In *Journal of the Warburg and Courtauld Institutes,* 9 (1946), 96–121.

KRAUTHEIMER, R., with T. KRAUTHEIMER-HESS. *Lorenzo Ghiberti* I, pp. 234ff.

PANOFSKY, E. *Renaissance and Renascences in Western Art.* Stockholm, 1960, pp. 123ff.

WHITE, J. *The Birth and Rebirth of Pictorial Space.* London, 1957. pp. 113–21.

WITTKOWER, R. "Brunelleschi and 'Proportion in Perspective.'" In *Journal of the Warburg and Courtauld Institutes,* 16 (1953), 275–91.

BRUNELLESCHI ARCHITECT

ARGAN, G. C. *Brunelleschi.* Milan, 1955.

FOLNESICS, H. *Brunelleschi.* Vienna, 1915.

FONTANA, P. "Il Brunelleschi e L'Architettura Classica." In *Archivio Storico dell'Arte*, 6 (1893), 256–67.

FABRICZY, C. v. *Filippo Brunelleschi, Sein Leben und Seine Werke*. Stuttgart, 1892.

GORI-MONTANELLI, L. *Brunelleschi e Michelozzo*. Florence, 1957.

HARTT, F. *History of Italian Renaissance Art*. New York, 1969. pp. 111ff.

HEYDENREICH, L. H. "Spatwerke Brunelleschis." In *Jahrbuch der Preuszischen Kunstsammlungen*, 52 (1931), 1–28.

KLOTZ, H. *Die Frühwerke Brunelleschis und der Mittelalterliche Tradition*. Berlin, 1970.

LOWRY, B. *Renaissance Architecture*. New York, 1962.

LUPORINI, E. *Brunelleschi, Forma e Ragione*. Milan, 1964.

MURRAY, P. J. *The Architecture of the Italian Renaissance*. London, 1963.

SAALMAN, H. "Filippo Brunelleschi: Capital Studies." In *Art Bulletin*, 40 (1958), 113–37.

SANPAOLESI, P. *La Cupola di Santa Maria Del Fiore. Il Progetto, La Costruzione*. Rome, 1941.

———. "Brunelleschi." In *Encyclopedia of World Art*, Vol. II. New York, 1960.

———. *Brunelleschi*. Milan, 1962.

BRUNELLESCHI'S TECHNOLOGY

BLUMENTHAL, A. H. "A Newly Identified Drawing of Brunelleschi's Stage Machinery." In *Marsyas, Studies in the History of Art*, 13 (1966–67), 20–31.

GARIN, E. "Mathematics and Science in Brunelleschi's Time." In "Brunelleschi," *Encyclopedia of World Art*, Vol. II. New York, 1960.

PRAGER, F. D., and G. SCAGLIA. *Brunelleschi. Studies in His Technology and Inventions*. Cambridge, Mass., and London, 1970.

PRAGER, F. D. "Brunelleschi's Clock?" *Physics*, 10 (1968), 203–216.

SANPAOLESI, J. "Ipotesi sulle Conoscenze Matematiche Statiche e Meccaniche del Brunelleschi." In *Belle Arti*, (1951), 25–54.

List of Illustrations

171